24 BLACKSMITHING PROJECTS

PERCY W. BLANDFORD

TAB BOOKS Inc.

Blue Ridge Summit, PA

FIRST EDITION
FIRST PRINTING

Copyright © 1988 by TAB BOOKS Inc.
Printed in the United States of America

Library of Congress Cataloging in Publication Data

Blandford, Percy W.
24 blacksmithing projects / by Percy W. Blandford.
        p.   cm.
Includes index.
ISBN 0-8306-2974-2 (pbk.)
1. Blacksmithing.   I. Title.   II. Title: Twenty-four
        blacksmithing projects.
TT220.B42   1988
   682'.4—dc19   88-4815
                                                          CIP

Questions regarding the content of this book
should be addressed to:

Reader Inquiry Branch
TAB BOOKS Inc.
Blue Ridge Summit, PA 17294-0214

1

Set of Punches and Chisels

A metalworker, whatever the particular branch of metalwork that interests him or her, needs a variety of punches and chisels. It might seem that there is never a large enough variety, that there are always different sizes and shapes that would suit a particular job better. Some of these tools also have uses, as they are or slightly modified, in working wood, leather, stone, and other materials. The blacksmith is able to make all these tools for his own or other craftsmen's use, even if his equipment is not as comprehensive as he would like. It should be possible to make most of the tools in this project with only a propane torch as a source of heat and an iron block as an anvil.

The material is high-carbon steel, which may be round, square, octagonal, hexagonal, or almost any other rod section. It need not be new and can be salvaged from discarded tools, springs, and similar things. Some commercially produced punches and chisels are made from special alloy steels. They need precise heat treatment unavailable to most individual blacksmiths, so these steels are better avoided. Ordinary high-carbon steel can be hardened and tempered satisfactorily with simple equipment.

A few punches, but not cutting tools, can be made from mild steel, which cannot be hardened and tempered, because it is unaffected by cooling in water. Remember not to do this with high-carbon steel; cooling in this way not only hardens it, but makes it brittle. Until you intentionally harden the steel it should be allowed to cool slowly.

Although short pieces of rod can be held with tongs, it is always easier to work on the end of a long rod, which can be held and then cut off. Where possible, do not cut the steel to length until after shaping its end.

If you wish to make something from high-carbon steel that has previously formed something else, it is advisable to anneal it to remove its temper and make it as soft and ductile as possible before reforging it. This is done by heating to redness and allowing to cool as slowly as possible. Leaving it in a fire overnight to cool is a good way of achieving ultimate softness.

A simple project is a center punch (Fig. 1-1A). Use rod of any section about ½ inch across. Draw down the end to about ⅛-inch diameter (Fig. 1-1B). Cut off to 5 inches long, and either forge or grind the top with a bevel all round (Fig. 1-1C) to minimize spreading when being hammered.

File or grind the tapered part to a bright finish. Finishing with emery or other abrasive cloth can follow, because the better the surface polish, the easier it is to see oxide colors when tempering.

Start from the end and heat about 1 inch to redness. Hold with tongs and plunge vertically into water (Fig. 1-1D). Be careful not to let the steel go in at an angle, which might cause cracking. Brighten the end again with abrasive cloth. This could not be done if it had not been previously polished; because the point would be very hard and brittle.

To temper, use a propane torch (Fig. 1-1E) or similar flame and heat between 1 and 2 inches from the point. Watch the spread of oxide colors towards the point. Heat will continue to spread, even when you take the flame away. The slower the heat, the greater the widths of the oxide colors, and the greater the width of steel at a particular temperature. The first color to reach the end will be a pale straw, which will deepen. When it has passed through dark straw to brown, plunge the point vertically into water. That should give a suitable hardness for a center punch.

An alternative method requires quicker action, but with only one heating. Have the tapered part bright and heat to redness as before, but only plunge a short distance into water. While the steel is still hot higher up, brighten the last inch and watch the spread of colors from the hot part. When you get the correct color, quench the steel completely.

If you let the colors go too far with either method, return to hardening before trying to tempter again. Most high-carbon steels can be hardened and tempered in water at room temperature. Some are intended to be quenched in brine (saturated salt solution) and some in oil. If you buy new steel, the supplier will indicate what to use. If you are re-using steel, and water causes the steel of a test piece to crack, use one of the other liquids.

For general purposes, grind the punch point to 60° (Fig. 1-1F). If the punch is intended to pierce sheet metal, as in traditional tinwork, the point may be 30° or up to 45°. For heavy work with a large punch, or for regularly locating the centers for drilling holes, an angle nearer 90° may be used.

Several center punches of different bulk and with different sizes and angles of points can be made. A fine punch with a long taper and small point forms a dot punch for locating spots (Fig. 1-1G). It could also be used for tinplate punching. A stone mason uses a rather longer center punch (Fig. 1-1H). A punch taken to a needle point (Fig. 1-1J) is used for piercing paper or leather. If fitted into a handle it becomes an awl. It could also be used as a scriber.

Punches for setting nails are made like center punches, but with ends square across (Fig. 1-1K). They could be hollowed by driving onto a ball bearing while hot (Fig. 1-1L). Make several, with ends from 1/16 inch upwards. High-carbon steel is advisable, but a nail punch of mild steel should have a reasonably long life.

You can make drifts like nail punches, but they will be longer and have a more gradual

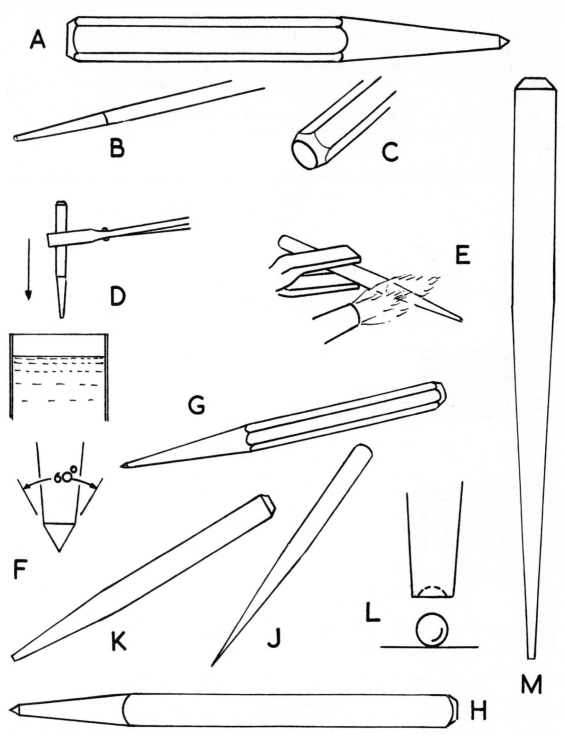

Fig. 1-1. Several types of punches can be made with basic equipment.

3

taper (Fig. 1-1M) for pushing through holes that should match and pulling them into line.

Chisels can be made almost like punches, using similar tempering colors. The sections of steel used will depend on the intended width of cutting edge. For light work you can use ⅜-inch rod, but ¾ inch or more is stronger and gives a better grip for heavy work. Length should be sufficient to get your hand around without hitting it; 6 or 8 inches would be suitable.

A cold chisel is used for cutting cold metals, and a hot chisel is used for hot metals. The only difference is that its cutting angle is more acute.

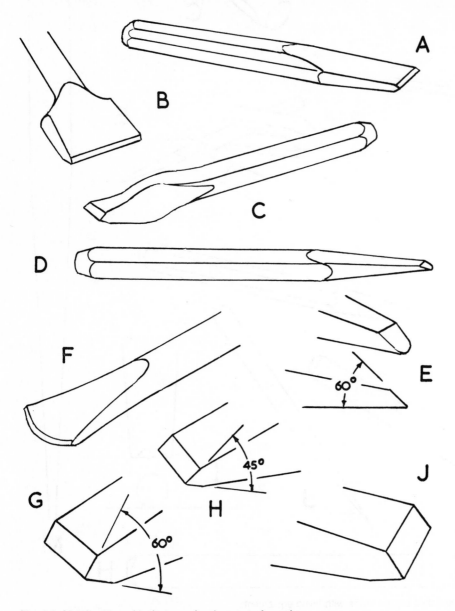

Fig. 1-2. Metal-cutting chisels are a development of punches.

4

A general-purpose chisel from ¼ to ¾ inch wide can be made by drawing down the end of a rod (Fig. 1-2A). If the cutting edge is to be wider than the body of the chisel, upset the end first. How much you upset depends on the final width (Fig. 1-2B). A cape chisel has a crosscutting form (Fig. 1-2C). Forge and file or grind this narrower behind the cutting edge so it does not bind when cutting grooves. Another type for cutting grooves with curved section is made something like a punch (Fig. 1-2D), but with a flat top surface and a cutting edge sloping to the curved side (Fig. 1-2E). For cutting corrugated sheeting or through other curves, the end of a chisel may be shaped (Fig. 1-2F).

With all chisels, brighten the ends for at least 1 inch so the tempering colors can be seen. Temper to about the same oxide color as punches. Do not grind the cutting edges until after tempering. For general purposes the edge of a cold chisel could be 60° (Fig. 1-2G), for regular use on soft metals it could be slightly less. The edge of a hot chisel may be 45° (Fig. 1-2H) or less. It is the contained angle that matters. For some purposes there might be more slope on one side than the other (Fig. 1-2J).

2

Wood-Cutting Tools

A large range of tools to cut wood, leather, and fabrics can be forged from high-carbon steel. Those that cut on their ends may be hardened and tempered in a similar way to the punches in the previous project. This type of heat treatment is suitable for ends up to about 1 inch across. For wider ends or knives, which have longer cutting edges, more complicated methods of heat treatment are advisable if an even temper at the edge is to be obtained.

A carpenter's simple marking knife has a cutting edge at one end and a point for use as an awl or scriber at the other end (Fig 2-1A). Rod $5/16$-or$3/8$-inch diameter is suitable. It would be possible to draw down the end to make a blade about twice as wide as the rod diameter by hammering directly, but it is better to upset the end first and make a wider blade. Cut and draw down the pointed end. In both cases do not go down to too thin a section. Hardening and tempering will be better if you leave a little for grinding to a cutting edge. Brighten both ends with as good a polish as you can get, then harden and temper each end separately. A brown oxide color should be right for the cutting ends. The idea is to leave the center part softer and tougher. Grind and hone both ends.

As a variation, use square rod and twist the center (Fig. 2-1B) for decoration and to provide a grip. In another variation, make the blade with a double angle (Fig. 2-1C).

A marking knife without an awl can be made from flat stock, that is drilled to take wood slabs as a handle (Fig. 2-1D). Steel $1/8$-by-$3/4$-inch section is suitable. Spread the end to make a wider blade. With the steel in a fully annealed state, drill two $3/32$-inch (or larger) holes for rivets. Harden and temper the end to a brown color.

The rivets could be a soft metal, such as copper. Drill the wood slabs slightly undersize and lightly countersink the holes (Fig. 2-1E). Cut the wire to extend far enough to allow

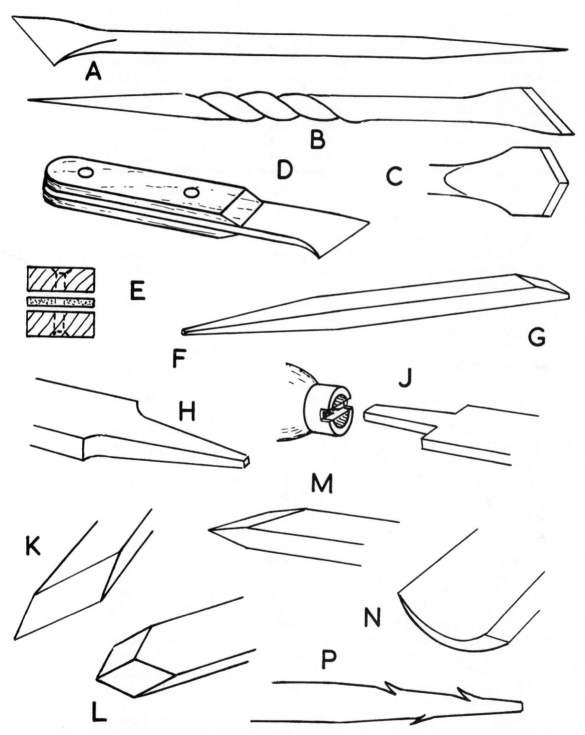

Fig. 2-1. Woodworking knives and chisels can be made from steel bar.

spreading into the countersinks. Rivet a little from each side in turn, with the handle supported on the anvil. Finally, file rivet heads and wood level. For further strength in the joints, put epoxy glue between the wood and metal before rivetting.

Wood chisels not intended to be hit, or to only be hit occasionally and lightly, may be made in a similar way to marking knives. Chisels smaller than those available from tool stores and with ends specially shaped will be welcome for carving and modelmaking. Chisels could be made from flat stock and given wood slab handles, but they are more convenient to use if they have tangs to fit into the more usual round handles. If you cannot make the handles, you can use file handles or pieces of dowel rod.

On each chisel draw down a tang to go into the handle—a length of 2 inches will be about right (Fig. 2-1F). At the other end grind towards the cutting edge, but leave a little thickness (Fig. 2-1G). The working end of the chisel should be smooth, particularly on the underside, so it can be honed to a good cutting edge. If you start with bright-drawn steel there will not have to be much smoothing, but otherwise, grind, file, and polish at least 2 inches from the end. Temper to a brown oxide color.

Chisels of this type can be made from $\frac{1}{16}$ inch square up to about $\frac{3}{8}$ inch square. For greater widths the stock need not be as thick. For instance, a $\frac{1}{2}$-inch chisel need not be more than $\frac{1}{4}$ inch thick. For wider chisels, reduce the width of the tang (Fig. 2-1H). For greater strength, square the shoulder at the tang, so the ferrule on the handle can be notched to engage with it (Fig. 2-1J).

The end of a chisel does not have to be sharpened straight across. It could be skew (Fig. 2-1K) either way, for carving. It could have a diamond point (Fig. 2-1L). There could be a bevel both sides for woodturning (Fig. 2-1M). Another woodturning tool has a stiff section, and is given an obtuse scraping angle for faceplate turning. Several such tools, with ends square and with different curves (Fig. 2-1N), will be useful to a bowl turner.

When tempering wider sections, keep the spread of oxide colors even by fanning the flame, around the body of the metal. Try to get the bands of color spreading parallel to the ends to achieve an even hardness there.

A carver might want the end of a chisel bent, because sometimes he pulls the tool to cut. A plain tang driven into a hole in wood might not offer much resistance to being pulled out. For these or any other pulling tool, cut teeth in the tang with a cold chisel (Fig. 2-1P).

If a chisel is intended for regular use with a hammer or mallet, a simple tang into a wood handle is not good enough because it would drive in further and split the wood. A chisel could be made without a handle (Fig. 2-2A), or it could have a slab handle (Fig. 2-2B). In both cases the steel takes the blow. A wood handle might go into a socket (Fig. 2-2C), but that is difficult to make. The alternative is a shoulder or bolster on the chisel to prevent it from going further into the handle (Fig. 2-2D).

Whether you can make chisels with bolsters or not depends on your skill and equipment. The tang part can be upset far enough back to form a bolster (Fig. 2-2E), then the tang drawn down (Fig. 2-2F). Another way is to forge the neck of the tang round and weld on a piece of thick-walled tube or drilled rod (Fig. 2-2G). In any case, you will have to finally shape the bolster with a file.

In general woodwork, gouges are not used as often as chisels. However, a turner needs gouges, and a carver's kit of tools might include 100 gouges.

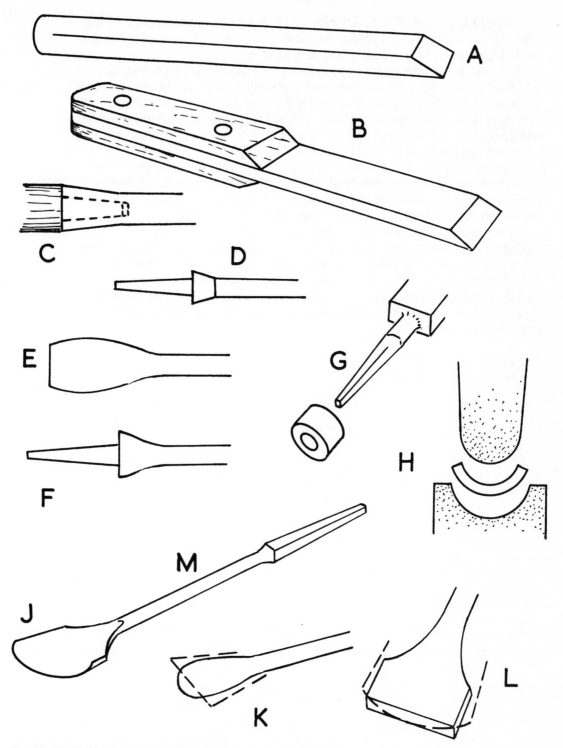

Fig. 2-2. Wood chisels may have slab handles or be made with tangs.

Making a long gouge of even section by hand is difficult, involving careful work with fuller and swage (Fig. 2-2H). Fortunately, a smooth inner surface for a great length is not so important, but the outside should be ground smooth.

For carving, many gouges have wider cutting ends (Fig. 2-2J). These spade gouges can be made in two ways. You can start with a rod and upset the end before spreading and curving it (Fig. 2-2K), then make a tang at the other end. The other way is to start with wider flat stock and reduce the neck. This will also lengthen it and you can finish with a tang (Fig. 2-2L). In both cases the tang should be square to prevent twisting, but at least part of the neck should be round (Fig. 2-2M).

Some spade tools have the neck or blade curved in the length—either up or down—and there might even be a double bend. Within each width a carver needs gouges of many different curves. The range of gouge shapes now available from commercial sources has been reduced considerably; this is where a blacksmith can step in.

Of the sources of high-carbon steel for re-use, old files seem an obvious choice for making chisels. However, care is needed. Files are sold almost fully hard, which means they are brittle. Do not be tempted to merely grind off the teeth and sharpen the end. When trying to use a file as a wood chisel, the edge would quickly crumble and if hit hard the tool might break, possibly with hazardous consequences. Before you make a chisel or anything else from an old file, anneal it, then harden and temper later to the condition that suits its use.

3

Garden Tools

Most hand tools needed in the garden can be made by a blacksmith, but some of the larger ones, such as spades and forks, would be difficult to make unless you have more advanced equipment than usually possessed by a smith. This leaves a large range of other tools, including some that could not be bought.

There is some sheet metalwork and a few joints that are better brazed than welded, but otherwise the work is straightforward forging of mostly fairly light sections. Mild steel can be used throughout, although high-carbon steel might be chosen for parts that have to cut or are liable to heavy wear.

Most tools need handles. You might choose to forge a tang to go into a hole in a wood handle. If the tool will be pulled, cut teeth in the tang (Fig. 2-1P) to strengthen the joint. Another good joint, particularly for attaching a long wood handle, uses a conical socket (Fig. 3-1A). Draw a view of the shape you want and repeat it each side (Fig. 3-1B). This gives almost a full circle and there can be a gap between the edges after shaping. If you want the edges to meet, allow a little more than three widths. Curve the ends. Appearance is improved if you shape the top. Shoulder the end of the tool to fit in the cone (Fig. 3-1C). Roll the cone to shape and weld it to the shouldered rod with the gap between the sheet metal edges underneath. Drill the cone for two or more wood screws into the handle. The choice of metal sizes depends on the tool, but for ½-inch rod the cone may be made of 16-gauge steel.

Where the tool if flat strip, there can be slab wood handles—as described in the last two projects. If you want to forge the handle as well as the tool, several shapes are possible, including some elaborate ones described in later projects. However, a decorative handle would be inappropriate for a utilitarian tool and could be rather heavy.

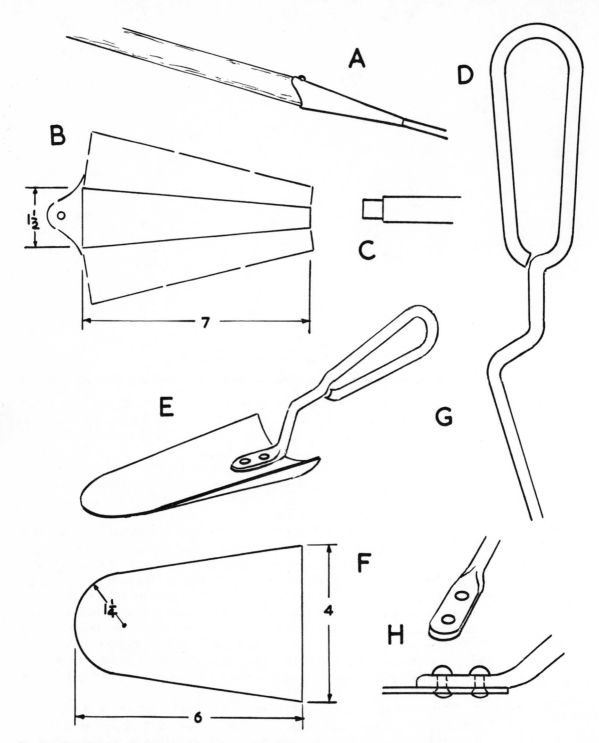

Fig. 3-1. A socket for a handle can be made or a handle formed with rod, as in this trowel.

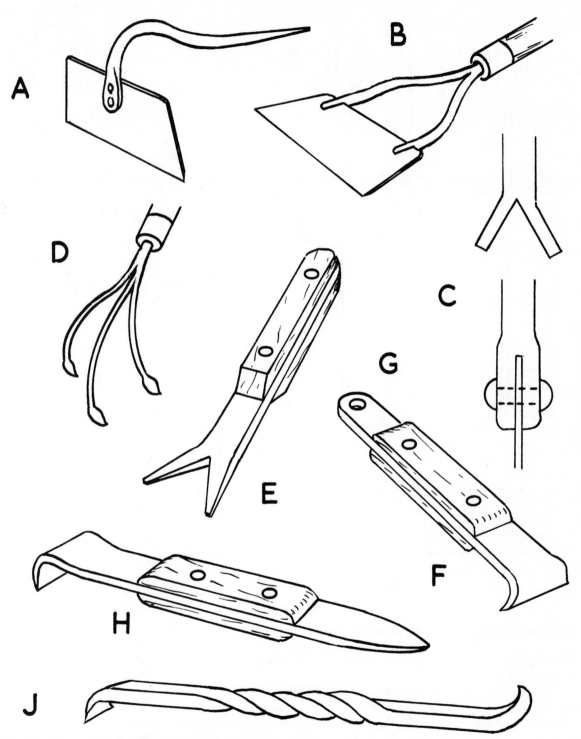

Fig. 3-2. Hoes and small garden tools are easy to make.

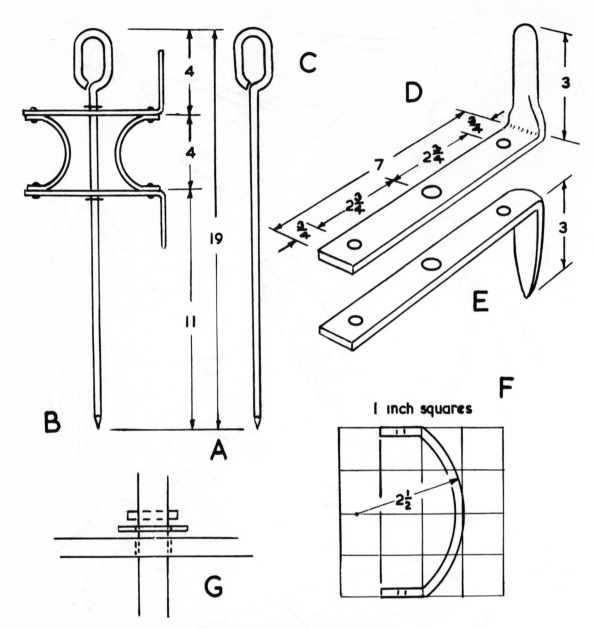

Fig. 3-3. A garden line winder has a spool on one spike.

A simple loop would be better (Fig. 3-1D). Make it long enough to grip and arrange it upright for most tools.

Trowels of several sizes are always useful. The example (Fig. 3-1E) is an average size, shown with a loop handle, but it could have a tang into a wood handle. Set out the blade, cut it out, and shape it (Fig. 3-1F). Rod ⅜-inch diameter will make the shaft. Shape the handle first, then make the double bend (Fig. 3-1G) before cutting off. Flatten the end for a sufficient length to allow for two 3/16-inch rivets (Fig. 3-1H). The joint can also be strengthened by brazing.

Several other tools can be made in a similar way. A hoe may be any width, and its 16-gauge blade is joined to a rivetted and brazed shaft (Fig. 3-2A), which can fit into a long handle or be arranged short for one-hand use. The blade could be straight, with a similar shaft, or you might prefer double shafts (Fig. 3-2B) brought together and welded. An alternative method of joining to the blade in either case is to split the rod end and open it so it can be closed over the sheet metal, where it may be rivetted and brazed (Fig. 3-2C).

A cultivator (Fig. 3-2D) may be made from 1/4-inch rod for one-hand use or from 1/2-inch or larger rod, and with a long handle, for heavy use. Upset the ends of rods to provide enough metal for hammering the shaped prongs. Weld the other ends together and reduce their size for attaching to a handle.

The end of flat strip, such as 1/4 by 1 inch, may be split to make a weeder (Fig. 3-2E), which can have a wood slab handle. A similar tool may have its end bent for scraping mud off other tools (Fig. 3-2F). Both tools could have their ends extended and be drilled for hanging or attaching to a cord (Fig. 3-2G). For work in boxes and pots, a double-ended tool is useful (Fig. 3-2H). For all these tools, draw the ends down to almost knife edges.

A similar tool made from flat strip and with a slab wood handle could be made with bent ends for getting weeds out of narrow gaps between stone slabs. Square rod might be used with a twisted center and the ends drawn down and angled opposite ways (Fig. 3-2J).

A garden line winder makes an interesting blacksmith project and is better than the two sticks and piece of string commonly used to get rows straight. There is a plain handled rod (Fig. 3-3A) and a spool for the line on another rod, with a handle for winding and a spike to push into the ground and maintain tension (Fig. 3-3B). The rods could be 5/16- or 3/8-inch diameter and the flat parts 3/16-by-3/4-inch or 1-inch strip.

Make the two rods the same. The handles could be round or lengthened, as shown (Fig. 3-3C). The points may be blunt squares, like nails.

The top and bottom strips are almost the same. The top strip is bent up and rounded to make a winding handle (Fig. 3-3D). The bottom strip matches, but its end is drawn down and bent to make a point to press into the ground (Fig. 3-3E).

Draw the shapes of the two spool pieces (Fig. 3-3F) and bend them. Drill top and bottom strips centrally to fit easily over the rod. Drill and rivet the strips together. They could also be brazed, but rivets alone should be sufficient. Allow for washers above and below the spool and drill through the rod for pegs, which are pieces of nails (Fig. 3-3G).

Garden tools are liable to rust. Treating with oil and heating will provide some protection, but paint is the best finish. Where a tool has a cutting or working edge, take the paint to within about 1 inch of the edge, then oil or occasionally clean the remainder with abrasive. This will enhance the appearance.

4

Plant Pot Hanger

This is a wall hanger to support a hanging pot. It is not as complicated as it might look; all the scrolls are based on one design. The bracket alone could be used to support other things, but a matching plant pot holder is shown (Fig. 4-1). Sizes will depend on the pot you intend to use and the size scrolls you can make—if you already have a scroll iron or other means of making matching scrolls. You could make C-scrolls instead of reversing them, without affecting the method of construction. The drawings are based on a pot about 12 inches diameter and 9 inches deep, and scrolls about 3 inches across (Fig. 4-2). Using scrolls of the type shown, anywhere between 2 inches and 4 inches across should make a satisfactory hanger, but you will have to draw a bracket shape and size to suit.

The scrolls may be made from ³⁄₁₆-inch-by-¾ strip and the frame from ¼-by-1-inch strip, but both sections could be reduced for a lighter construction and ease in working. The pot holder may be the same section strip as the scrolls. A pot full of wet soil is quite heavy, so do not reduce steel sections too much.

The scrolls could be pulled round with fork tools, but it is easier to get uniformity with a scroll iron made of slightly stouter strip than the scrolls. Shape its outside to what will be the inside surface of a scroll. Thin and widen its inner end for hooking on the scroll strip, and turn down the other end to grip in a vise. Draw half a scroll (Fig. 4-3A) fullsize to get the shape. Some parts will use only a section of the shape.

With the fullsize drawing as a guide, lay out three scrolls as you want them in the bracket (Fig. 4-2A). They are shown at 45°, but you could alter the angle slightly if you wish. Outside the scrolls draw the line of the bracket. Although this is your intended size, it is advisable now to make the three scrolls and join them, because the frame

Fig. 4-1. A plant pot hanger with scroll decorations and a frame around the pot.

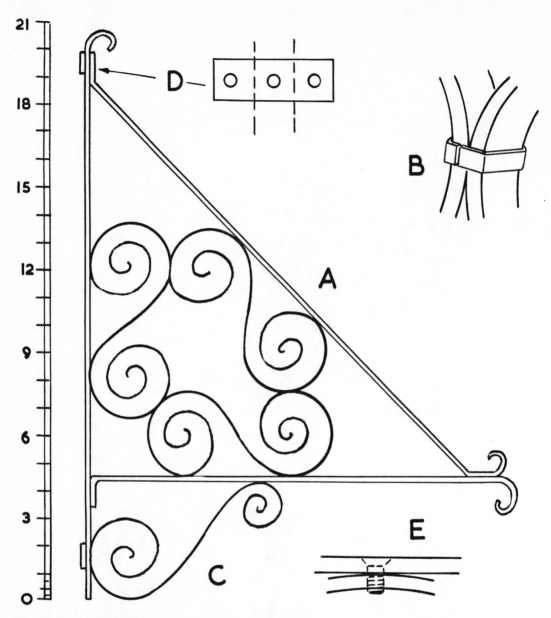

Fig. 4-2. Suggested size and arrangement of the hanger bracket.

size might have to be adjusted to suit the overall size they finish.

The simplest way to join the scrolls is by spot welding. They could be brazed. Another way is with a metal collar (Fig. 4-2B), which need only be about 1/16 by 1/4 inch and bent cold.

Lay out the framing strips to fit around the scrolls. Check that the arm is square to the back. Bend the ends to fit against each other. At the top and extending ends make smaller scrolls (Fig. 4-3B).

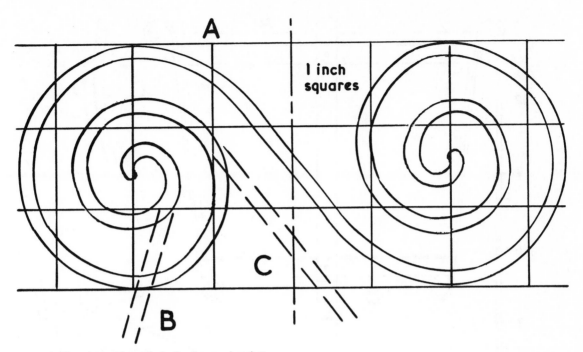

I inch
squares

C

B

Fig. 4-3. The shape of scrolls in the hanger bracket.

Make the supporting scroll (Fig. 4-2C) with one end to the same size as the inside one, but at the other end use only part of the shape (Fig. 4-3C). Arrange its angle and length so it touches the arm clear of the inside scroll. Make two short pieces for attaching to the wall (Fig. 4-2D).

It would be possible to weld all the bracket parts, but screwing is suggested, using ¼-inch countersunk screws (Fig. 4-2E). Attach the arm to the back, with a screw from the rear. Locate the supporting scroll and drill for screws through the back and the arm. At the back, take the screw through the attachment piece. Screw downwards into the scroll from the arm.

Put in the three joined scrolls. Screw them through the framing. At the same time join the frame parts and include the other attachment piece at the top.

The size of the plant pot holder depends on the pot to be used. The top ring goes around the pot ½ inch or more below the rim of the pot (Fig. 4-4A). The bottom ring is below the pot (Fig. 4-4B). Arrange the ring diameters to allow the pot to fit easily. The strips used could merely have overlapping joints, but it will be better to joggle them (Fig. 4-4C) so the inside surfaces are level. Join with a rivet or a screw, as in the bracket. Arrange the joints to come between the uprights.

The uprights are all the same. They might have the shorter scroll ends (Fig. 4-3B), although you can increase the amount of scroll if you wish.

To support the pot make two crossing pieces (Fig. 4-4D) to fit inside the circle (Fig. 4-4E). The slight unevenness where they cross at the center will not matter, because pots are usually hollow in the bottom and supported on their rims.

19

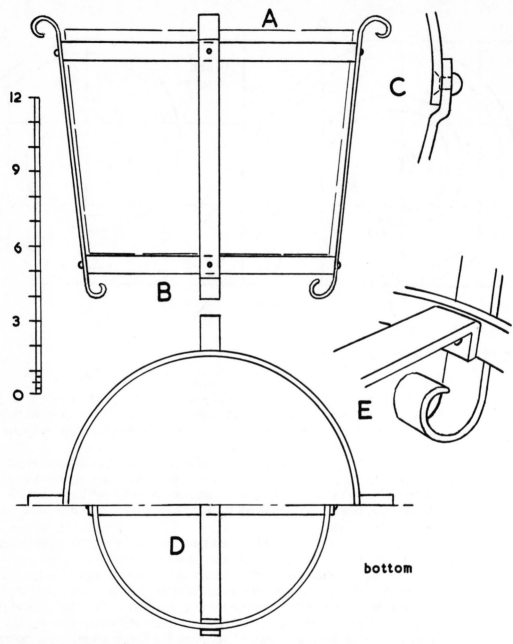

Fig. 4-4. Details of the hanging pot holder.

Mark all the hole positions on the uprights together, and mark the holes equally around the rings so they assemble without twist. All the parts of the pot holder could be joined with rivets, or have countersunk heads inside and round heads outside. Screws could also be used in the same way as in the bracket, except there might be round heads outside.

20

5

Plant Stands

A stand made of mild steel can hold one or more pots of plants indoors or on a patio. With a painted finish it will look attractive in itself and complement the display of foliage or flowers. Several variations are possible. There could be three or four legs; designs with three are described. They have the advantage of standing steady even when the surface is uneven, but four legs can be arranged with very little alteration to the method of construction. Besides the stand for a single pot (Fig. 5-1 and 5-2A), there could be two or more pots supported at lower levels (Fig. 5-2B) or shelves might be fitted (Fig. 5-2C) so other arrangements besides pots could be displayed.

The forge work involves scrolls, bends, and twists. Joints may be rivetted, screwed, or welded. The legs should be ¼-by-¾-inch bar or stouter. Other parts may be the same or could be thinner, but the stand will look best if they are the same width. For indoor use it might be satisfactory to make the whole stand of lighter sections. Bar with rounded edges will give a lighter appearance than square-edge stock.

The scrolls could be the same as in the last project (Fig. 4-3), or any other similar size for which you have a scroll iron or other shaping arrangement. Set out the legs (Fig. 5-3A). Make one or two twists, depending on the stand being made. A 360° twist should be satisfactory (Fig. 5-3B). Form the scrolls and see that all legs match.

If the top is to hold a pot, this will determine your sizes, but there might be ample clearance, so pots could be changed later. Make a ring with its ends welded or overlapped and screwed or rivetted (Fig. 5-3C). The supports are three pieces with scrolled ends (Fig. 5-3D), that fit over the leg and cross and meet at the center under the pot. Allow some excess length so you can cut and match the parts at the center. The three evenly spaced pieces may be cut and welded (Fig. 5-3E). They could be overlapped and screwed

Fig. 5-1. A strip steel plant pot stand
for use indoors or outdoors.

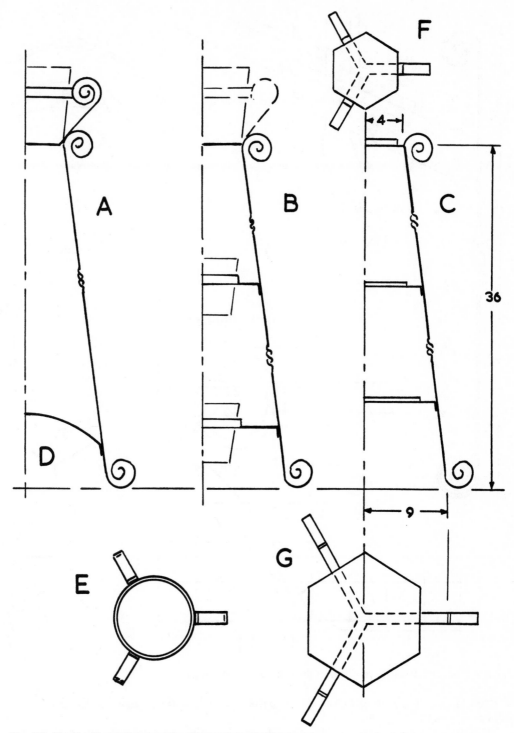

Fig. 5-2. Sizes and variations on the plant pot stand design.

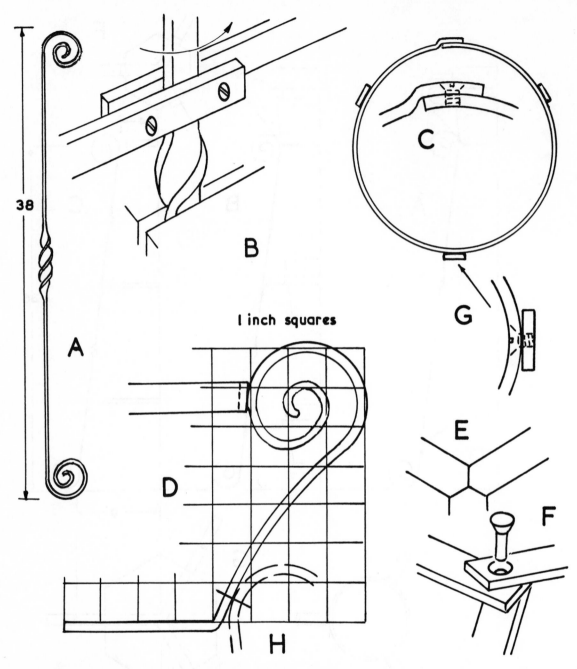

Fig. 5-3. Sizes and details of variations of the plant pot stand design.

or rivetted (Fig. 5-3F). In that case, let the parts slope down to the center so the pot will be supported at its rim.

For the stand for a single pot, there are three rails between the lower parts of the legs (Fig. 5-2D). They are shown with curves up to where they join at the center, in one of the ways described for the top. Join to the legs with screws or rivets.

At the top, join the ring to the evenly spaced scrolls with screws driven outwards (Fig. 5-3G). Do the same at the meeting with the leg scrolls (Fig. 5-3H).

Assemble the stand without rivets or screws fully tightened, so you can check, by viewing from a distance, that a pot will be level and the legs are without twist. Finally

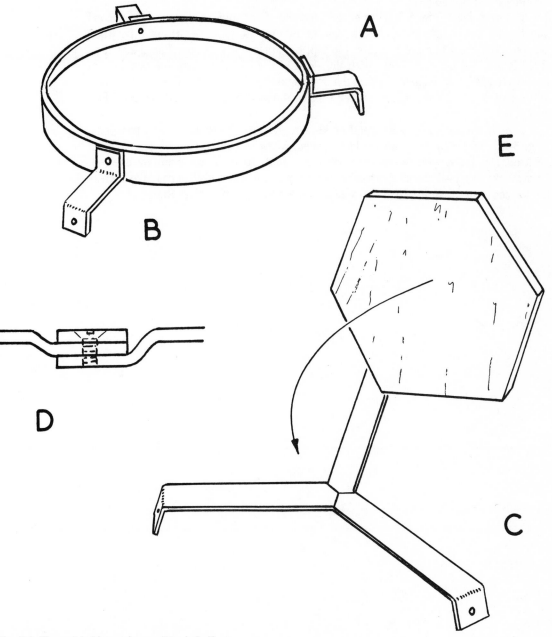

Fig. 5-4. The pot holder and an optional shelf.

tighten the joints and finish the metal with paint.

If two or more pots are to be supported (Fig. 5-2B), the lower ones will be held by rings. Make each ring to fit under the pot rim or about one-fourth of the pot depth down if there is no rim (Fig. 5-4A). Set out a side view of the stand with the positions the rings are to be marked. From this get the sizes of struts to the legs (Fig. 5-2E and 5-4B). As with the first stand, make an untightened assembly to check accuracy before tightening and painting.

The third stand (Fig. 5-2C) has shelves instead of pot holders. This and the second stand could have single twists in the legs, or two twists might be arranged between shelves. You could fit a pot holder at the top, but shelves are shown (Fig. 5-2F) at all three levels. Set out a half view with the slope of the legs and mark the positions of the shelves and their supports. From the drawing make the supports (Fig. 5-4C). Weld at the center or joggle the pieces so their tops will be level when screwed together (Fig. 5-4D).

The shelves could be solid wood or ½-inch plywood. They are shown hexagonal (Fig. 5-2G and 5-4E), but they could be round. Sizes should be about 1 inch in from each leg. Drill the supports so three woodscrews can be driven upwards into the shelves. Because the wood will absorb more paint than the steel, it is advisable to paint the shelves before screwing them in place. They could be a different color than the steel.

6

Yard Seat

Steel makes a good framing for a seat that is to be kept outdoors, but it is not comfortable material to sit on. Wood is much better for parts in contact with the body. If treated with preservative or painted, it will have a reasonably long life. For the structural parts steel is stronger and more durable, particularly if the seat is to remain outdoors for most of the year. Its weight also provides steadiness, so there is little risk of inadvertently tipping the seat if it is not attached to the ground.

A seat can be made for one, two, or three persons. Construction is the same. This seat or bench (Fig. 6-1) has about 48 inches of seat length, so it is suitable for two. As drawn, most parts are made of ½-by-1½-inch bar, but sections could be reduced a little for a lighter assembly and ease in working if your source of heat is limited. With the sections shown, this makes a seat that is intended to be put in position and stay there almost indefinitely.

The wood parts are all 1½-by-3-inch section and 54 inches long, with the outer edges well rounded. Choose a straight-grained hardwood. If the metal parts are painted and the wood given a clear oiled or varnish finish, the result will be very attractive.

The key parts are the two ends (Fig. 6-2A), which are made of single pieces following around (Fig. 6-2B), with arms attached (Fig. 6-2C).

Set out the shape with the aid of 3-inch squares. The places where the underframing parts are attached should be vertical (Fig. 6-2D and E). The arms attach between the back wood slats. Thickness is reduced where the arm joints come, and the feet are also reduced and spread.

When shaping, you will probably find it best to start at the rear to reduce the length of bar projecting from the fire as quickly as possible. Spread the end for the foot (Fig. 6-3A). When you have made all feet, you might have to file them to match.

Bend the top curve and follow round the shape, so you finish by forming the front

Fig. 6-1. A yard seat with wood parts on a steel framework.

foot. Make the second end to match the first.

Shape the two arms. At the back reduce the thickness for neatness (Fig. 6-3B). You could punch both the arm and the back for ⅜-inch or ½-inch rivets, which will spread both parts and give a typical forged appearance (Fig. 6-3C). Alternatively you could drill for rivets. If you prefer, you could bolt through or cut threads and screw the joints. At the front, taper the arm end and join to the leg in the same way as the back.

The underframing is made up of ¾-inch square rods at the ends and two rails meeting

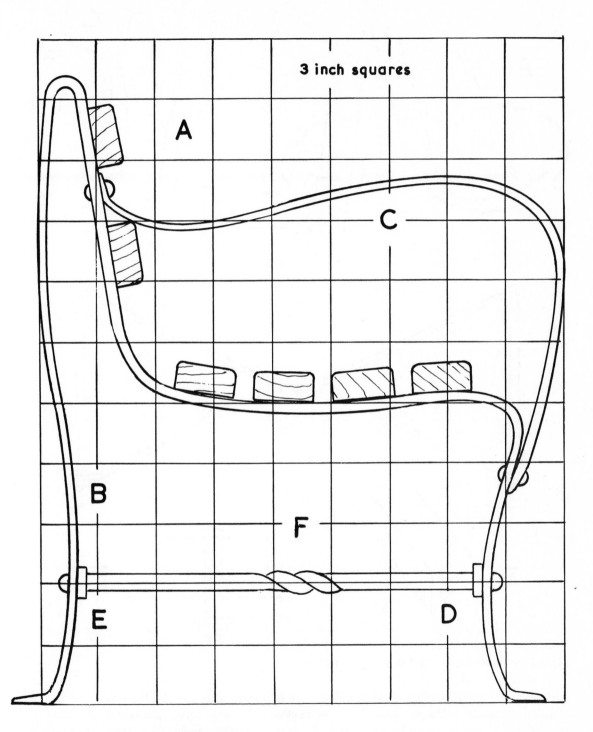

Fig. 6-2. The shape to make the yard seat ends.

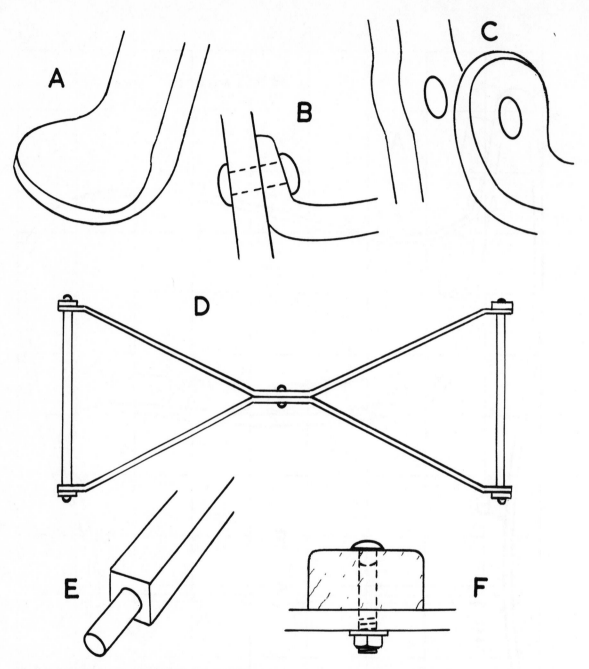

Fig. 6-3. Details of seat parts and its underframing.

at the center (Fig. 6-3D). They could be the same section as the ends or ⅜-by-1½-inch rod. Relate the size of the rail assembly to the lengths of the wood parts. Allow for a parallel part to rivet at the center and ends to fit under the rivetted rods. Allow some excess length until you have drilled or punched the ends. Put a twist at the center of each rod (Fig. 6-2F) if you wish. Shoulder the rod ends to ½ inch for sufficient length to go through two thicknesses and form a rivet head outside (Fig. 6-2E). Punch or drill the holes.

A single ⅜-inch carriage bolt should be sufficient everywhere wood crosses metal (Fig. 6-3F). Drill the steel ends to take the bolts.

Assemble the underframing to the ends. Stand the assembly on a flat surface. Clamp the top back rail in position and check squareness, by measuring diagonals. Check that the ends stand upright. See that all four feet are taking the weight and the assembly is free from twist. When you are satisfied, drill the top rail and bolt it on. This should hold the assembly in shape so you can mark the holes in the other pieces of wood and bolt them on.

7

Trestles

Supports that can be moved around and used for more than one purpose can be valuable. In a workshop such a trestle can support work that overhangs the end of a bench, or it can keep it level as it comes off a machine. Two trestles could support a table top, then the parts put away when not needed. They might be used under stout boards to make a temporary bench or a platform to stand on when working at a moderate height. There are many occasions when you want to raise the project you are working on so you can avoid having to stoop. Trestles can be made to various heights, but the most useful ones are about table height.

Some of the trestles described here are light ones, primarily intended for use under a table top, where they are not connected together except by the table top. Another trestle folds flat, but is more rigid if it is to stand independently. It could be used alone for the end support of long work. A pair may be used under boards for a platform or for working on long, heavy material. Where it is expected that the trestles will be used mainly to support a platform of loose boards, it is stronger and safer to brace them to each other, so the structure is rigid.

The first design (Fig. 7-1A) could be used singly, but it is intended mainly for use as a pair for forming a table with a wood top. Sections used will depend on the intended use. If you only want a light table, such as for food preparation at a barbecue, you could use strip ¼ by 1 inch and ½-inch (or even lighter) rods. If you expect to do heavier work, ⅜-by 1¼-inch and ⅝-inch diameter would be better.

The two uprights (Fig. 7-1B) have spread feet (Fig. 7-1C), which could be made by welding parts together, or you could rivet them (Fig. 7-1D).

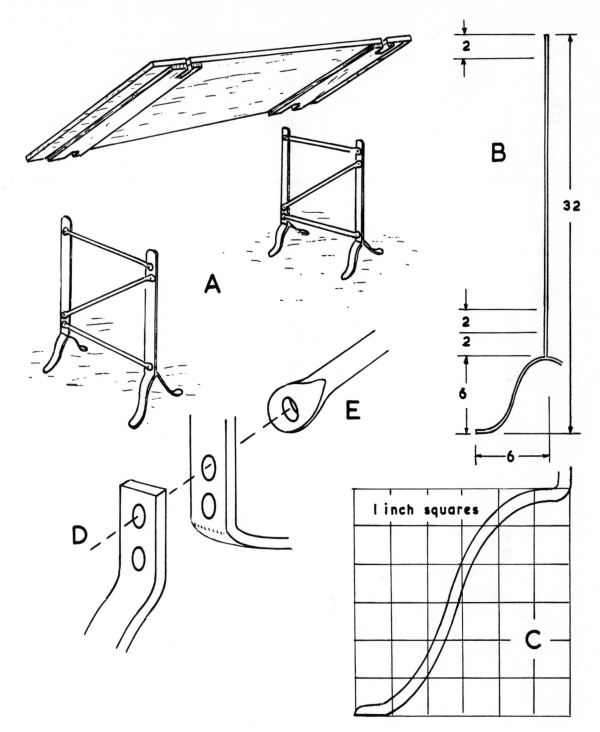

Fig. 7-1. Trestles suitable for supporting a table top.

33

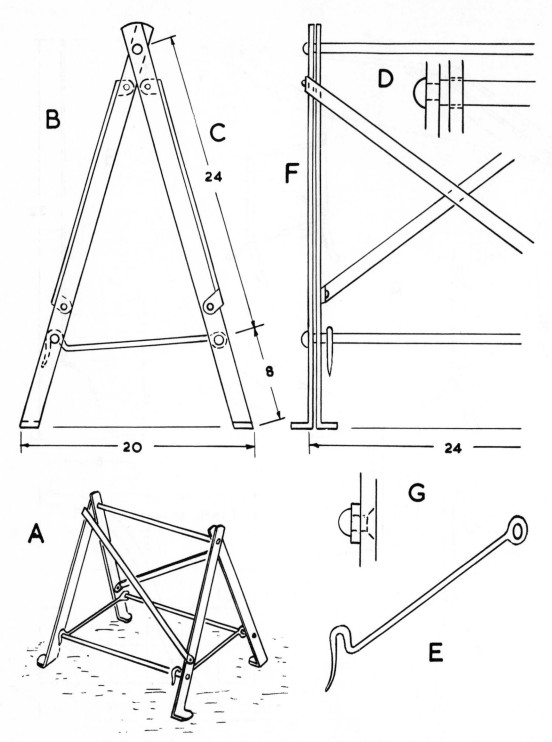

B

C

24

F

D

20

8

24

A

G

E

Fig. 7-2. A stable trestle that will fold flat.

Prepare the rods with flattened ends large enough to take ⅜-or ½-inch rivets or bolts (Fig. 7-1E). Mark the uprights for the holes to take the horizontal rods. At the top allow sufficient extension to pass through slots in the wood table top, but to not quite reach the surface. A suitable top might be made from four boards ¾ by 6 inches, cut to the length you need, with crosspieces made from the same section wood. Cut the slots to fit easily over the metal.

Rivet or bolt the horizontal rods to the uprights and square the assembly. Put the diagonal brace in position and mark through the holes in the legs.

The fold-flat trestle is held stable and rigid by two large hooks (Fig. 7-2A). The sections you use depend on the strength needed, but ⅜-by-1¼-inch strip for the uprights and ⅝-inch diameter for the rails can be braced with ¼-by-1-inch diagonals, for a trestle that should stand up to average use. As shown (Fig. 7-2B), there is a 24-inch top rail about 30 inches above the floor.

The four uprights are the same (Fig. 7-2C), except the feet are turned in on the inner pair and out on the outer pair, so as to allow closer folding. Delay drilling until the other parts are made.

Shoulder the ends of the top rod to ½ inch, so it may be taken through the outer uprights and rivetted (Fig. 7-2D). Make bottom rails the same, except for the inner one, which is shorter to give clearance between the frames. The inner rod joints would be better with countersunk rivet heads. Drill the uprights for the rod ends and clearance holes at the top of the inner uprights.

Make the two hooks from ⅜-inch rod (Fig. 7-2E). Make the ring to fit fairly close on the ⅝-inch rod. Make the hook end deep, so there is little risk of it being knocked off when the trestle is locked open, and taper and curve its point for ease in fitting.

Assemble the parts made so far. Check squareness by measuring diagonals. Make the two braces. One goes outside the outer uprights and the other fits inside the inner uprights (Fig. 7-2F). Drill the ends and put them in place to mark through the holes in the uprights. Countersink the holes on the sides towards the other uprights (Fig. 7-2G), so the rivet heads will not interfere with folding the trestle as closely as possible.

A trestle assembly could be made with the ends braced to each other to give strong support for a platform or temporary bench. The two ends can be made like a part of the fold-flat trestle, with lengthwise bracing added. An alternative method of construction is shown in Fig. 7-3A. There are no round rods, but the rails and brace at each end are formed from single pieces of flat strip (Fig. 7-3B). This involves careful bending and you will have to work from a fullsize setting out. The section to choose depends on how strong the trestle needs to be, but ⅜-by-1½-inch strip throughout should be adequate support for a temporary bench for heavy use, or a platform for one or more persons to stand on. Rivets may be ⅜ inch and the bolts for the lengthwise bracing could also be ⅜ inch, preferably with butterfly nuts.

The four uprights (Fig. 7-3C) should have turned-out feet, which could be thinned and spread. Round the tops. Delay drilling rivet holes until you have bent the internal pieces, in case there are minor variations to allow for.

Drill for the bolts to the lengthwise bracing (Fig. 7-3D). You might wish to cut threads to screw them in or weld them in place to avoid the risk of losing loose bolts.

Clamp the parts of one end together. Check squareness and drill through for rivets.

8

Outdoor Table

A well-painted, all-steel table can be left outdoors almost indefinitely without suffering much from extremes of climate. It is then always ready for use. If you prefer, the table could have a wood top, with all other parts steel. This table (Fig. 8-1) has an octagonal top 42 inches across. At the center it could hold the pole of a large umbrella. There are four legs of decorative shape, with scrolls that provide strength as well as decoration. The top is sheet metal with a rim stiffened with angle iron. Exterior plywood could be substituted without affecting the construction of other parts.

Start by laying out a half side view showing one leg complete (Fig. 8-2A). Suggested section for the leg strip is ⅜ by 1½ inch. The angle iron may be 1½ by 1½ by ⅜ inch. The flat strips under the 10-gauge sheet top are ⅜ by 2 inch. The added scrolls may be the same section as the legs or thinner. The lower plate that carries the second hole for the umbrella pole is ¼ inch thick. Bend the strips for the four legs (Fig. 8-2B). Make one and use it as a pattern for the others. Leave a little extra at the end of each top, to be trimmed later during assembly. The scrolls could be any size for which you have a scroll iron or other shaping device. Those shown are all the same and 4 inches across.

Make the eight double-C scrolls (Fig. 8-2C and Fig. 8-2D). You could also form them as S shapes if you wish. In any case, the joining part looks better curved than straight.

Cut the strips that cross under the top (Fig. 8-3A). Their top surfaces must be level. One piece can be joggled under the other (Fig. 8-3B), and there could be a joint cover screwed underneath (Fig. 8-3C). If you have welding facilities, the joint could be welded (Fig. 8-3D). Drill for the umbrella pole; this will probably be about 1¼-inch diameter.

Make the lower ¼-inch plate (Fig. 8-2E and 8-3E), 13 inches across and octagonal. Make a matching hole at the center. Mark where the legs will overlap, and at a point

Fig. 8-1. An octagonal table for use outdoors.

central under the upper scroll positions, mark screw holes. Position each upper scroll, then mark and drill for countersunk screws, with threads cut in the scrolls (Fig. 8-3F). Locate the lower scrolls and drill similarly for screws at the lower positions (Fig. 8-2F). It will not be possible to use screws under the central plate. Leave these joints until last when you assemble, then weld the scrolls to the plate, or it might be possible to braze them.

Assemble the four legs, their scrolls, and the lower plate—with the assembly inverted on a flat surface. Adjust the legs so they are square across. When you are satisfied, clamp on the crossing 2-inch pieces. Mark for holes. You could join with countersunk screws and nuts (Fig. 8-3G), or use rivets in the same positions.

Mark out the top octagon on what will be the underside of the sheet metal (Fig. 8-2G). Leave trimming to the exact size until after the angle iron frame has been bent, in case there are slight variations in size or shape.

With the marked octagon as a guide, cut and bend the angle iron (Fig. 8-4A). Perfectly

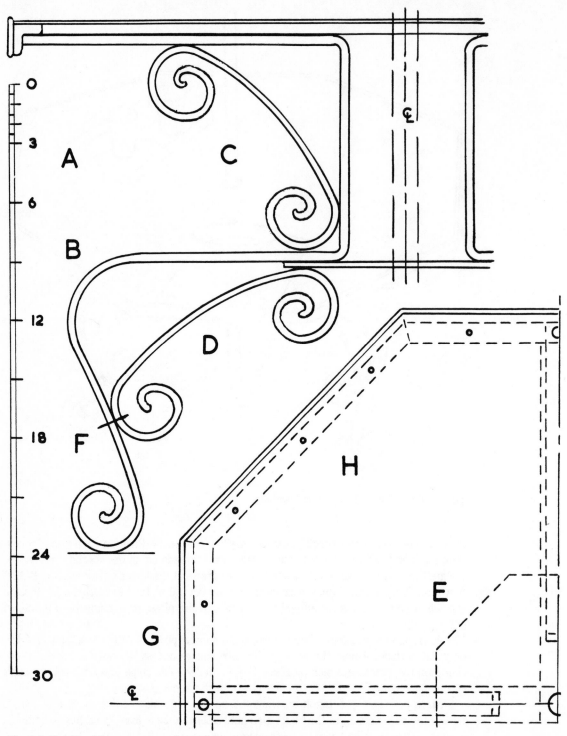

Fig. 8-2. Details of the supports and top of the outdoor table.

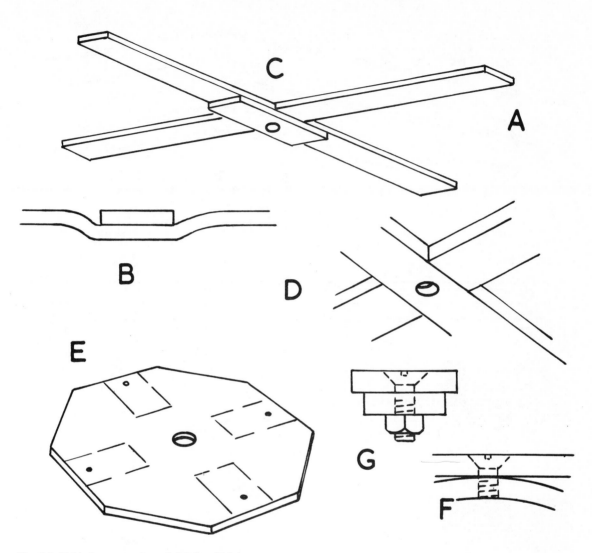

Fig. 8-3. Table top supports and details of joints.

matching joints might not affect the finished shape, but cut them as neatly as you can. It should be sufficient to put three $\frac{3}{16}$-inch countersunk rivets along the four unsupported sides (Figs. 8-2H and 8-4B), but the bolts into the legs may take the place of one rivet on each of the other sides. Arrange an even spacing around the top.

Trim the sheet metal level with the angle iron. Cover the edge with strip, preferably with rounded edges (Fig. 8-4C). Rivet or screw it to the angle iron.

The top is attached to the leg assembly with eight countersunk $\frac{1}{4}$-inch bolts. Arrange four at the ends of the legs, which are cut to fit closely into the angle iron (Fig. 8-4D), and four just inside the vertical bends of the legs (Fig. 8-4E).

Remove any sharpness on the steel edges. Remove any rust, then treat with rust-inhibiting fluid, if possible, and give all surfaces several coats of paint.

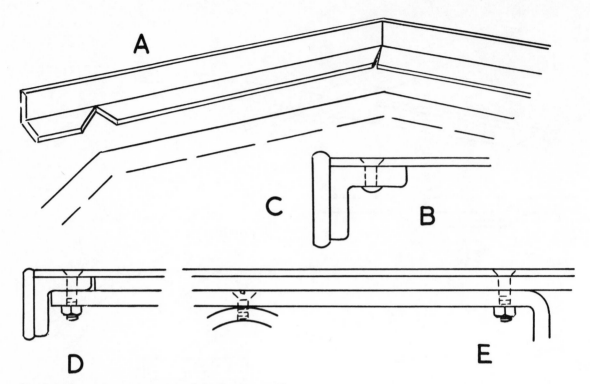

Fig. 8-4. The angle top supports and details of assembly.

9

Glass-Topped Table

If furniture made of metal is to hold its own alongside the more usual wood furniture, it has to have a fairly light and more delicate appearance than many general blacksmithing projects. It can have ornate shapes and curves, particularly scrolls, so the parts are an expression of the maker's artistic intentions as well as his practical ability.

This table (Fig. 9-1) has the ironwork supporting a glass top. The glass should be clear or tinted, sufficiently transparent for the shaped steel to be viewed through it. Sizes will depend on the glass disc. The suggested size in the drawing is a 20-inch disc of ¼-inch glass with the edge rounded and polished. The table height could be the same as the glass diameter.

Sections of steel depend on the strength required, but this table should not have to stand up to much rough treatment. However, the parts must hold their shape in normal use. The supporting structure could be strips ³⁄₁₆ or ¼ inch by 1 or 1¼ inch. The parts under the glass could be ⅛- or ³⁄₁₆-inch by ¾-inch strip. With the lightest sections it might be possible to make some curves cold, if you have suitable rollers. Otherwise, the circular rim and other parts may be formed to a drawing or template.

The apparently complex assembly can be broken down into units, which may be made independently before being brought together. The parts enclosed in the circular rim are one unit. Two opposite legs are made as one piece, joined across at the bottom. The feet under them also go across. The legs and feet the other way are separate and linked to the continuous assemblies with rivetted straps.

Set out one half or one fourth of the top (Fig. 9-2A). The steel circle is 1 inch in from the edge of the glass. Each C scroll occupies one fourth of the circle, so draw lines

Fig. 9-1. This glass-topped table shows the ornamental steelwork through the glass.

through the center at 45°. Within each sector the centers of the scrolls come on a 5½-inch radius. Draw a scroll so it will touch the circular rim and the neighbouring scroll. The details of the scroll can match any existing scroll iron you have.

Form the circle. Its ends could be welded to make a continuous ring, or one end may be given a double bend to fit inside the other and be rivetted. Make the four C scrolls. Fit them into the circle, adjusting their curves as necessary so they touch each

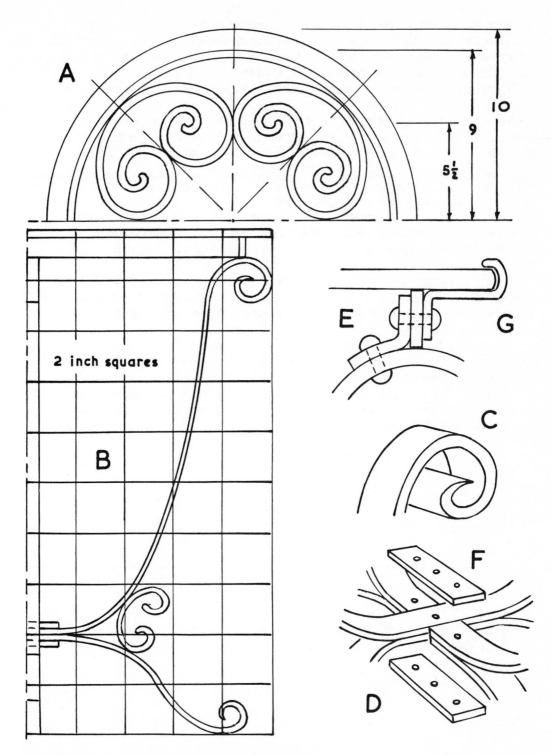

A

10

9

5½

2 inch squares

B

E

G

C

F

D

Fig. 9-2. Shapes and sizes of parts of the glass-topped table.

other and the rim. So the glass top is supported without rocking, it should rest only on the circular rim. Check that the edge in contact with the glass is flat. When you attach the scrolls, keep their upper edges slightly low. The fact that they are up to $\frac{1}{8}$ inch lower than the rim will not be apparent in the finished table.

If you have facilities, weld the scrolls to each other and to the rim. Otherwise drill for rivets or screws.

Set out half the shapes of legs and feet (Fig. 9-2B). If you make one of the sides, it can be used as a pattern for the opposite half and the doubled sides. Appearance will be improved if the inner ends of the scrolls are thinned and spread (Fig. 9-2C). Do this at the tops of the legs and ends of the feet. The ends of the small C scrolls are not so important. As you form the legs and feet allow for a flat area at the joint, sufficient for cover straps about 3 inches long (Fig. 9-2D).

Check the size across the continuous pair of legs under the rim. Spring in or out, if necessary. Make four angle brackets (Fig. 9-2E) to take $\frac{3}{16}$-inch rivets through the scroll and rim. Drill for these brackets and rivet them to the four leg scrolls only at this stage.

Temporarily clamp each leg to its foot so you can position a small C scroll and weld, rivet, or screw it in place. Drill the top cover strap for $\frac{3}{16}$-inch rivets (Fig. 9-2F). Bring the parts together to mark and drill through. Be careful to keep the crossing square as you tighten the rivets.

At the top the glass has to be held in position to prevent it from being lifted off inadvertently. This is done with a light strip metal clip at each leg joint (Fig. 9-2G). Strip $\frac{1}{16}$- by-$\frac{3}{8}$-inch section would be suitable. Make each clip with its outer end well rounded. At first have it standing up or only slightly turned in. When you fit the glass, squeeze the clip end lightly over the glass with a clamp or vise. However, finish the steel with paint before finally fitting the glass and closing the clips.

10

Pokers

Most people expect a blacksmith to produce pokers. Even today, when open fires are less common, there is a demand for pokers, if only to hang on a wall. Pokers offer scope for decoration, and a poker is a self-contained, satisfying piece of forgework that does not require much metal.

Because pokers have been made for centuries, all possible designs must have been employed. The designs suggested here are all based on tradition. Most can be varied in several ways, so the range of possible designs is almost infinite. Someone with artistic ability might spend considerable time forging an animal head handle, or something similar. The following designs are more utilitarian, but they are attractive in their functional appearance.

Rod should be ⅜-inch diameter upwards, but ½ inch or more might be heavier than most users would want to handle, particularly if the poker is long. For use with wood fires, the length could be anything from 24 to 48 inches. If there is no particular requirement, an overall length of 30 inches is reasonable. Some pokers are better made of square rod. Many pokers can be made without welding, but the ability to make a fire weld is important if you want to make a more advanced poker.

A simple poker, such as might be used by the smith himself, has an eye forged at the top (Fig. 10-1A). The other end could be simply pointed, but it will look better and stand up to use in the fire better, if it is first upset, then a short square point forged (Fig. 10-1B).

The loop handle does not have to be round. It could taper (Fig. 10-1C), be elongated (Fig. 10-1D), or be given any shape you wish (Fig. 10-1E). The eye can be left with

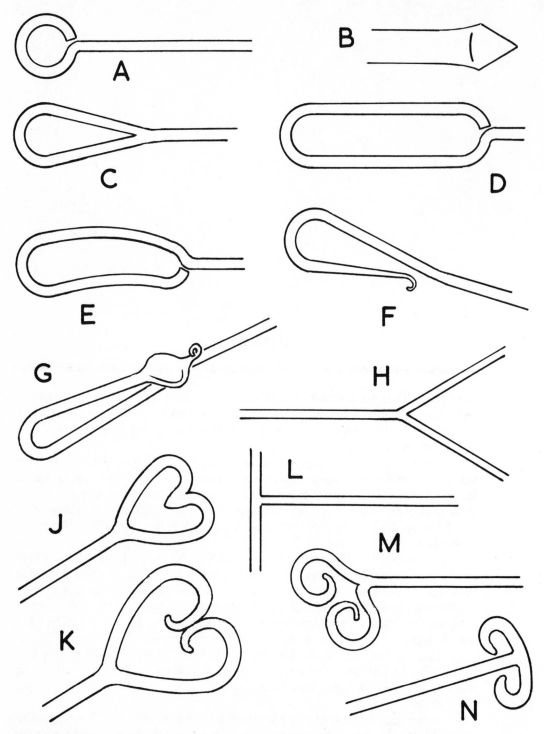

Fig. 10-1. Poker handles offer scope for a large range of designs.

the rod end close to the shaft—which is functional, but it is a better display of your skill to weld the meeting close.

An open loop looks better if the end is drawn down before the bend is finished. A popular handle then looks like a shepherd's crook (Fig. 10-1F). A variation on this has a thumb grip (Fig. 10-1G). To get sufficient metal to make a broad thumb spot, upset first, make the thumb spot, then draw down the remaining end. This is best made with a fairly close loop. Experiment with your fingers around a loop and your thumb on the spot.

Several designs are possible if you weld two pieces together (Fig. 10-1H). A double loop can have the ends turned down the inside to give a more solid handle. A popular traditional double loop forms a heart (Fig. 10-1J). The heart could be developed with the ends drawn down and small scrolls included in the handle (Fig. 10-1K).

If you start by welding a T piece across (Fig. 10-1L), other variations are possible. The obvious ones are scrolls upwards (Fig. 10-1M) or downwards (Fig. 10-1N).

If you twist a round rod there is no apparent difference, but if you twist a square you get an interesting helix. The neck of a round poker may be filed square for about 2 inches (Fig. 10-2A). Heat it evenly and you get an even twist (Fig. 10-2B). Beware of uneven heating; you will get a tighter twist at the hotter part, which might not be what you want. Of course, if you start with a square rod you can put a twist in the poker at any point and for any reasonable length. It is difficult to get an even twist over a long length.

In another form of twist, the handle end is drawn down for a considerable length, then a loop formed and the remaining end wrapped around the neck of the poker (Fig. 10-2C). With two or three rods welded together (Fig. 10-2D), it is possible to twist them together like rope, then weld their ends to make a thicker handle (Fig. 10-2E). In a variation of this, sometimes called a "blacksmith's twist," use more thinner rods (four will do) and twist them in the same way. The welded end can be carried on to make a small hanging hook or loop. Heat the twisted part and untwist it to open as a comfortable cage handle (Fig. 10-2F).

A handle could be in the form of a knot. You could reduce the diameter of the rod for the amount needed. A knot will have to be made in a fairly open form first. You cannot merely pull through, as you would rope. When the necessary turns are all included, close up progressively to get a compact knot handle. The figure-8 knot shown (Fig. 10-2G) is simple to make.

There is an advantage in having a long thick square end to the poker: it gives good resistance to possible overheating in the fire. Upsetting a round rod sufficiently to forge it square would require many heatings. It might be better to start with square bar and swage it down to round (Fig. 10-3A). A ½-inch square rod could be left fullsize for a few inches, then the rest reduced to ⅜-inch diameter.

For dealing with logs in a wood fire, it is sometimes necessary to pull instead of push. This can be arranged by welding a spur a short distance back from the working end (Fig. 10-3B). There might be an advantage in curving the forward point as well (Fig. 10-3C). A second spur for pushing can come opposite or at a different position (Fig. 10-3D).

Double prongs will make the poker into a fork. A simple V shape (Fig. 10-3E) is not as effective as a curved fork with parallel prongs (Fig. 10-3F), which will lift as well as push logs. A single-pronged poker can be curved like a fork prong (Fig. 10-3G), but

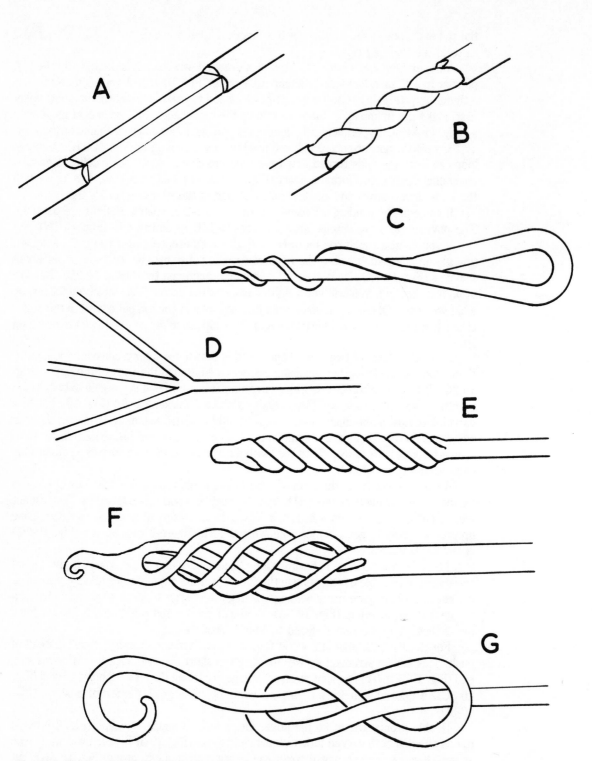

Fig. 10-2. Twists can be included as decorative features in pokers.

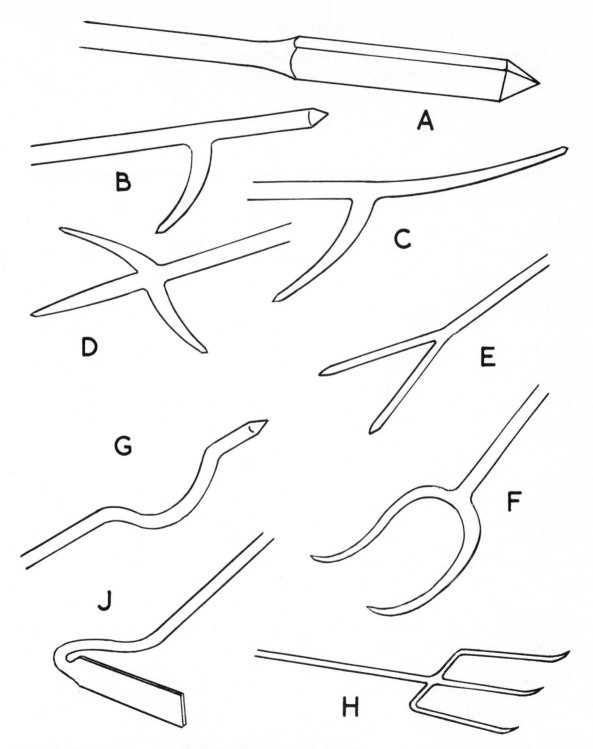

Fig. 10-3. There are many ways of fashioning the working end of a poker.

it will obviously not be as effective in lifting logs. A lighter version of the poker/fork could serve as a toasting fork, with two or three prongs (Fig. 10-3H).

At a domestic hearth there is a need for a rake to pull ashes. It is very similar to that used by the smith (Fig. 10-3J), but with an ornamental handle to match other fire tools.

11

Door Hinges

In the past, a blacksmith was expected to make hinges for many purposes. For a traditional appearance, forged hinges are still very effective, particularly for a closet, room, or larger outside door. Other door hardware (see next project) can be made to match, which gives an effect very different from that of plastic and mass-produced metalware.

Forged hardware is more appropriate for larger sizes, so it is best avoided for such things as small cupboards and boxes, unless you want to do more delicate work with small metal sections that could mostly be formed cold. Sheet steel not less than ⅛ inch thick and pivot pins at least ³⁄₁₆ inch diameter are typical for forged hinges. This means strap hinges about 12 inches long and other hardware in proportion. The hinges described here will suit a fairly large and heavy interior or exterior door.

There are two main types of surface-mounted traditional hinges: the strap or T hinge (Fig. 11-1A) and H hinge (Fig. 11-1B), with its variation the HL hinge (Fig. 11-1C). The extension of the strap and HL hinges provide strength across the grain of one or more boards. In the past, strap hinges were shaped and decorated in many ways.

An undecorated strap hinge will show the method of arranging its pivot. For ⅛-inch plate the pivot could be ¼-inch rod. It is helpful to have a longer ¼-inch rod with its end drawn down (Fig. 11-1D) to form knuckles round, then the pivot rod is not driven in until the hinge is assembled. The ends of a hinge pin could be lightly rivetted over, but it is usual to merely cut off the rod level. The center part of the strap at the knuckle may be about 1½ times as wide as each part beside it (Fig. 11-1E).

Allow sufficient length of the strap end to wrap round the rod (Fig. 11-1F). The other part should extend more to clear the center wrap (Fig. 11-1G) after that has been

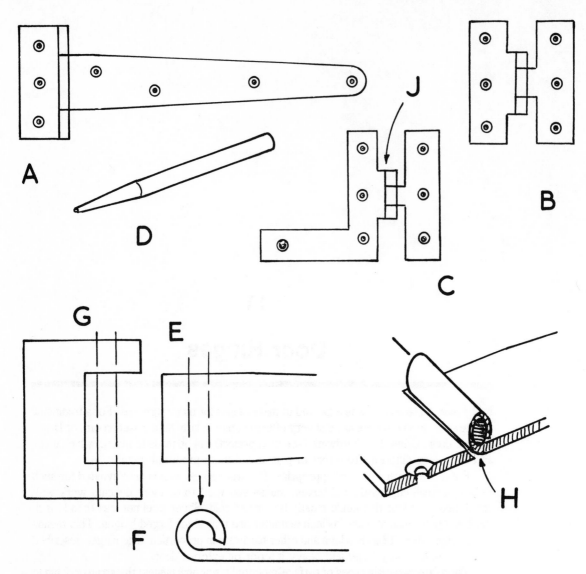

Fig. 11-1. Surface-mounted hinges can be strap, H, or HL, with knuckles formed around rod.

fitted. If you want a closer fit, the gap can be made tighter and the metal filed (Fig. 11-1H). Holes in both parts may be staggered, so as not to come in the same wood grain lines and run the risk of splitting.

Hinges may be decorated by chopping shaped outlines, welding on pieces, hammering the edge or all over with a ball-peen hammer for a dappled effect, or grooving with a fuller. Some examples are shown in Fig. 11-2.

H and HL hinges can have their pivots formed in a similar way to strap hinges, but it is usual to extend the pivots (Fig 11-1J). This brings the screwed parts far enough from the edge of the wood to reduce the risk of grain breaking out. The projecting part of an HL hinge may be any length. Some older ones are long enough to serve as straps

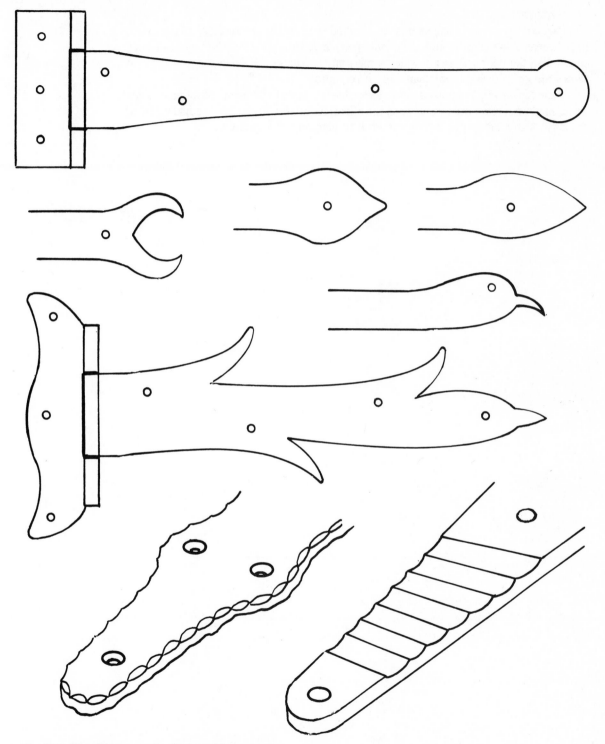

Fig. 11-2. Strap hinges can be decorated in many ways.

to hold boards together.

Parts of any of these hinges may be cranked to allow for the surfaces of doors and their frames being at different levels. Both parts may be cranked so the knuckle stands clear, then the door will swing wide to miss an obstruction. Raising the knuckle also allows a door to swing more than 180° if required.

If the hinges are being used for an assemble intended to be a reproduction of older work, modern screw heads would spoil the effect. Nails with forged heads could be used, or raised screw heads could be hammered to give an aged appearance.

12

Door Latches and Bolts

In addition to hinges, a blacksmith was expected to provide fasteners for doors. Blacksmiths made graceful and attractive latches and bolts that are worth reproducing today, particularly for doors hanging on forged hinges. Substantial forged steel latches and bolts are more effective and attractive for exterior doors than the often fragile pressed steel or plastic fittings available today.

The simplest latch (Fig. 12-1A) can only be operated from one side of a door, although a string may be attached and taken through a hole above to be pulled from the other side. For two-sided operation there has to be a thumb latch (Fig. 12-1B). In either case the latch may be a piece of ⅛- by 1-inch parallel strip about 12 inches long. A pattern of lines chopped on it is a traditional decoration (Fig. 12-1C). The end of the latch could be forged to make a round pivot (Fig. 12-1D). A shouldered rivet into a back plate will allow easy movement (Fig. 12-1E).

The cranked strip that holds the latch close to the door and restricts its movement must be long enough to allow the latch to lift at the striker plate. It could be made from ⅛-by-½-inch strip and is better with a flat piece behind it (Fig. 12-1F), to prevent wear on the surface of the door.

The striker plate arrangement depends on the doorway. A flat striker plate can be let into the side of the door frame (Fig. 12-1G), or one can be mounted on the surface (Fig. 12-1H). In both cases, slope the front so when the latch hits it, it will ride up and drop into the socket.

The lever to operate the latch from the other side is usually incorporated in a handle (Fig. 12-1J). Fingers go round the handle so the thumb comes in a convenient position to press down on the flattened end of the lever. A matching handle may be made, with-

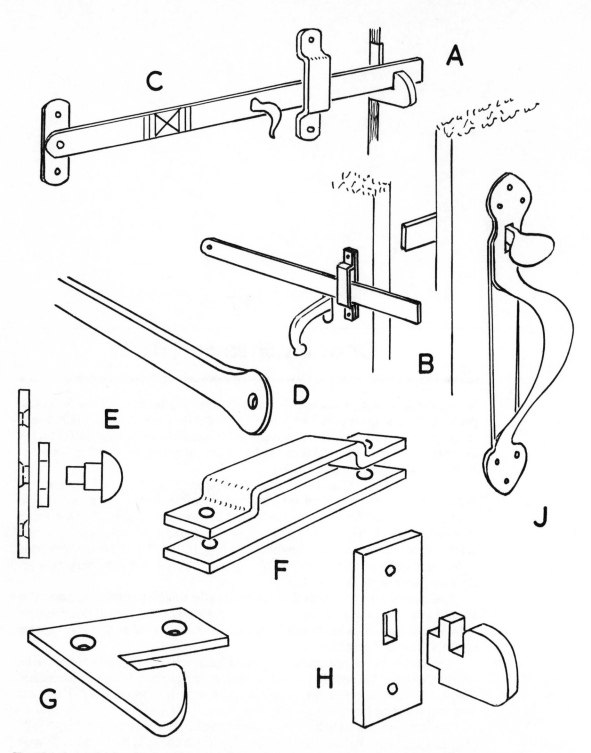

C   A   B   D   E   F   G   H   J

Fig. 12-1. A door latch engages with a catchplate and can be operated from one or both sides of the door.

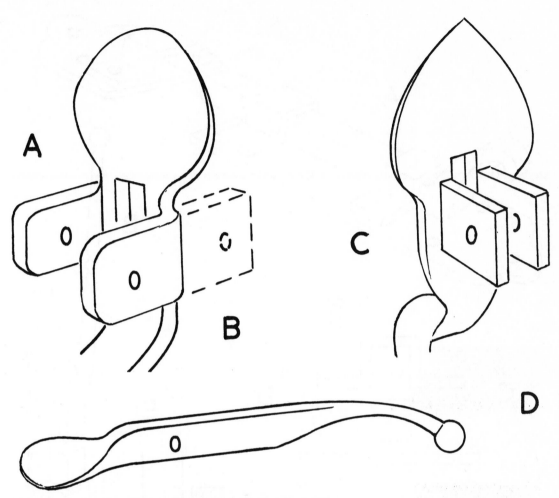

Fig. 12-2. The lever to operate a latch pivots on lugs on the handle.

out the lever, for the other side of the door. The only problem with making a handle with the thumb piece conveniently close is providing a pivot for the lever. One way to do so is to use sheet metal and bend two arms outward (Fig. 12-2A) or inward to let into the thickness of the door (Fig. 12-2B). The second arrangement requires less thrust by the thumb, because of the shorter leverage under the latch. If you forge a solid handle two pieces may be brazed or welded on, either in front or behind, with a ⅛-inch diameter pin through (Fig. 12-2C).

Forge the lever from 3/16- or ¼-inch-by-½-inch strip. Make a broad palm for the thumb, either flat or hollowed. Taper the other end to a curve to go under the latch (Fig. 12-2D). Many shapes for the handle are possible, besides the loop shown.

A bolt to secure a door may be made to work horizontally or go up or down near the edge of the door. It may go into a hole in the floor or the door surround, but it will more likely need a catch plate. The bolt assembly can be decorated to match the hinges and latch. The handle end of the bolt provides scope for ornamental shaping.

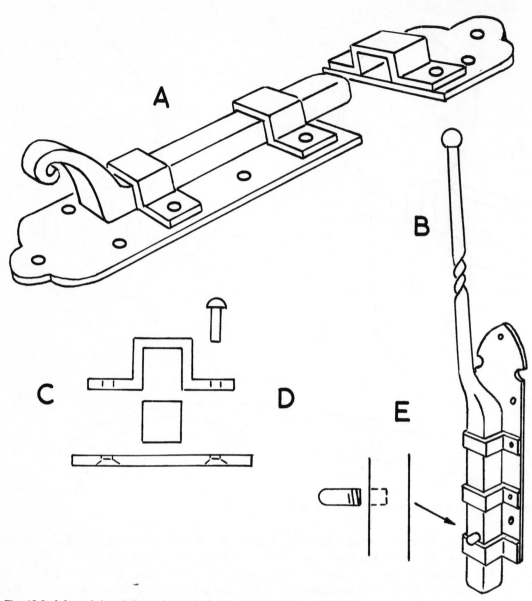

Fig. 12-3. A forged door bolt can be made for use horizontally or vertically.

For an average door, the bolt itself can be made from ½-inch square rod. There could be a short loop handle (Fig. 12-3A), formed as a scroll or any other way you wish. If the bolt goes up or down and there is a long reach, you can make a long handle with a knob or other decoration (Fig. 12-3B).

Shape straps to fit over the bolt (Fit. 12-3C) and one with a little more clearance to go on the catch plate. Allow for rivets into the back plates (Fig. 12-3D). This will control the minimum width you make the plates. Decorate the back plate to match the hinges and handles. To limit bolt movement, put a pin in the bolt to act as a stop (Fig. 12-3E) when it hits the straps. It could be brazed in a hole or threaded to screw in. Screwing would allow you to disassemble the bolt, if ever necessary.

As with the hinges, attach the latch or bolt with forged nails or screws disguised to look old, if you are doing reproduction work.

13

Simple Wind Vane

A wind or weather vane is as much a decoration as a practical indication of wind direction. There is almost unlimited scope in the choice of design, which might be functional, symbolic in some way, or comical or whimsical.

Size has to be related to height above the observers. Some wind vanes on church steeples are so large and heavy it is surprising that wind has enough power to move them. Some of these large and high wind vanes have considerable detail, which seems a waste of the blacksmith's's skill and art when it is too far away to be seen. For a one- or two-story house, the wind vane can be much more compact. General details are within view, but there is nothing to be gained by including fine detail. Your wind vane has to be planned for its general effect. There is a temptation to make a wind vane too small. Even if you only want to put the vane on a small building in the yard it should be about 24 inches across the letters, with a total height very nearly the same.

A wind vane needs a large area to one side of the pivot, so that it blows around like a flag away from the wind (Fig. 13-1A). There can be area forward of the pivot to complete the design, but this must be relatively small. The relative areas are also affected by their distance from the pivot: area further out is more effective than close in (Fig. 13-1B). Together with the problem of area comes the need to balance weights. If the vane is to turn easily, the weights each side of the pivot must be reasonable well balanced. This is often arranged by having the end into the wind longer and putting a weight, in the form of an arrow head, on the end (Fig. 13-1C).

If you design your own wind vane, try to get about twice as much of the area affected by the wind on the downwind side and enough weight with minimum windage on the other side to put a balanced load on the pivot.

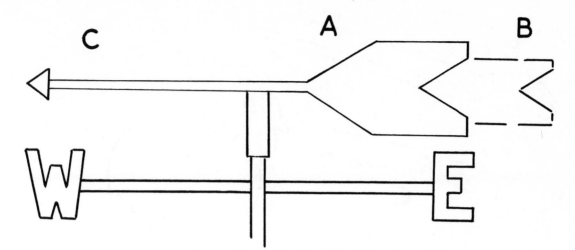

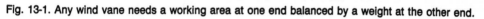

Fig. 13-1. Any wind vane needs a working area at one end balanced by a weight at the other end.

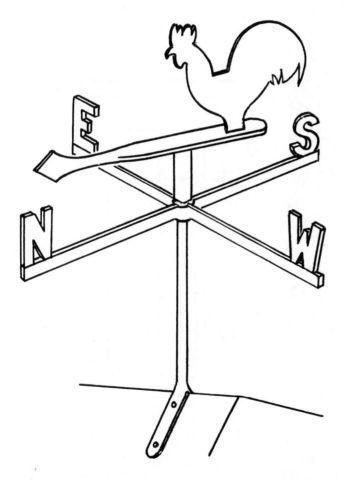

Fig. 13-2. A simple wind vane with a traditional cockerel.

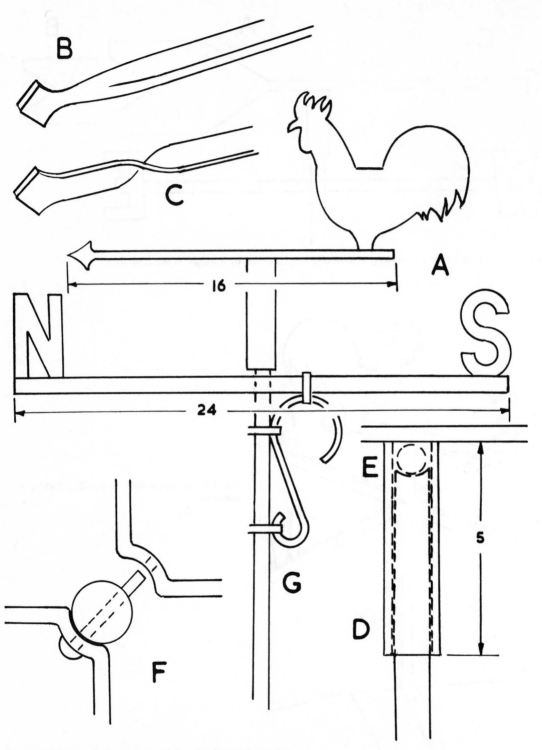

Fig. 13-3. Details of construction of the simple weather vane.

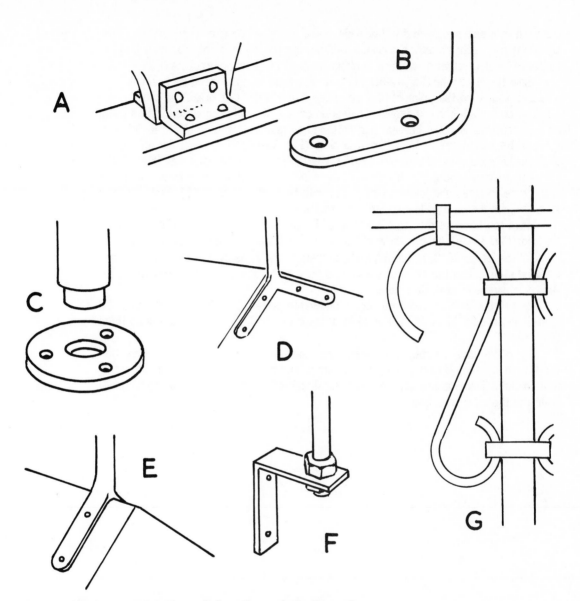

Fig. 13-4. Wind vane construction and alternative methods of mounting.

In this basic design (Fig. 13-2) the rotating part is supported on a ball. Weather vanes are sometimes known as weather cocks, because in the past a cutout of a cockerel was often used to provide windage on the vane. Some of these on church steeples have the cock almost central, so are not very effective. This one places the cock, or other symbol, away from the point of balance.

Make the bar (Fig. 13-3A) from ¼- by 1¼-inch section. There is a choice of points. The bar may be kept flat and an arrow head forged (Fig. 13-3B), or it may be twisted to make it easier to form an upright arrow head (Fig. 13-3C).

Draw the cock or other shape on steel plate, ⅛ inch or more thick. The cock shown will fit in an 8-inch square and will provide ample windage. Chop or burn out the shape and file it true. Aim to get a reasonable outline, but precision is not essential. Join the cutout to the bar, either by welding or by using sheet metal angle brackets (Fig. 13-4A).

Make the pivot tube (Fig. 13-3D). Use stout-walled tube that makes an easy fit over a ¾-inch rod. Find the point of balance of the bar and weld or braze the tube there.

The central ¾-inch rod details will depend on how it is to be mounted. If it is going on a flat surface, it could be bent and flattened to take screws or bolts (Fig. 13-4B). It might be shouldered and rivetted to a plate (Fig. 13-4C). To mount flat on a gable there could be flat wings fire-welded on (Fig. 13-4D). Joined on the other way (Fig. 13-4E) they will go above the gable. If you want the wind vane to stand away from a wall, the rod can be screwed and joined to a bracket with two nuts (Fig. 13-4F). Make the rod with either a flat or a hollow top to support the ball (Fig. 13-3E).

Make the arms from ¼-by-¾-inch strip. Form them in pairs, shaped to fit against the rod (Fig. 13-3F), where they will be joined with two ⅛-inch, or thicker, rivets.

Cut the letters N, S, E, and W, and join them to the arms by welding or using small rivetted straps. Join the arms to the rod so they come about ¼ inch below the tube. Adjust squareness in all directions.

Appearance is improved with scrolls under the arms (Fig. 13-3G). They could be quite light section: ⅛ by ¼ inch or ⅜ inch would do. Make straps to go around them (Fig. 13-4G).

If possible, give the steel a rust-inhibiting treatment, then a thorough painting. Bed the ¾-inch steel ball in thick grease, and assemble and try the wind vane before mounting it in position. Take care to get the rod vertical and, or course, make sure the compass points in the right direction!

14

Ornate Wind Vane

Some wind vanes on older European buildings were beautiful examples of the blacksmith's skill. Many of them are still working after centuries of use. They would have been made of the now almost unobtainable wrought iron, which has a good resistance to corrosion after forming the initial layer of rust. Mild steel is more vulnerable, but if treated with a rust-inhibiting fluid and well painted, it should have a long life even if exposed to the elements.

This project (Fig. 14-1) is based on a design perched high on a turret of an English castle. The original was about 10 feet high and 6 feet across. This scaled-down version could be mounted on your roof, but it would look good and make your workmanship more apparent to visitors if it was mounted on a pole somewhere that the wind is not screened, so the vane can perform its primary function correctly as well as decoratively.

The original wind vane was surmounted by the coat of arms of the owner of the castle. That and the four letters were finished in gold, which glinted in the sun, against the black of the rest of the ironwork. The assembly will be quite satisfactory without anything special at the top, but you could use the badge of any organization or even invent your own coat of arms.

As drawn and described, this wind vane involves some fairly advanced smithing, including many fire welds, the making of leaves, and some careful matching and fitting. The scrolls and other decorative work come in all four directions of the fixed part of the wind vane. You could make a simpler version, using the scrolls but omitting some of the more complicated flourishes.

For the sizes suggested (Fig. 14-2) the central pillar is made of 1-inch square and 1-inch round rod, the arms are ¾ inch square, the scrolls in the fixed part are ⅜ by

Fig. 14-1. An ornate wind vane based on a traditional design.

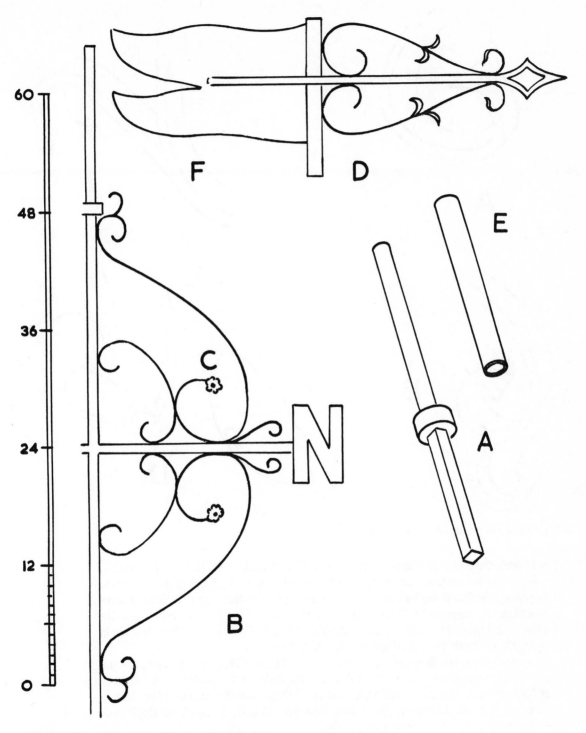

Fig. 14-2. Sizes of the parts of the ornate wind vane.

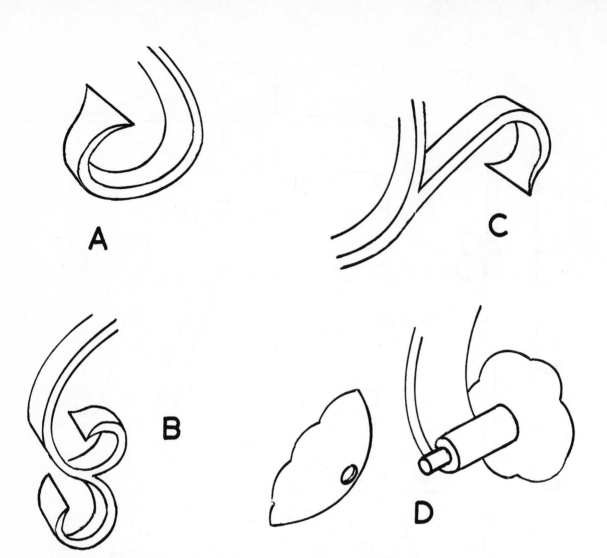

Fig. 14-3. Scroll details for the wind vane.

1 inch, while the main vane parts are reduced to ⅝-inch square and ¼-by-⅝-inch strips.

Start with the central pillar, using 1-inch square bar up to the collar at the top scroll. Allow enough length at the bottom for attaching to a pole or other support. Several ways of mounting are suggested in Project 13. Weld on a piece of 1-inch round rod to provide the pivot, and strengthen this with a collar (Fig. 14-2A). The pivot will be a ball, as in Project 13, so finish the top of the rod flat or hollow.

Set out fullsize the shape of the fixed part (Fig. 14-2B). The scroll patterns are the same above and below the arm. From this drawing make all the scrolls. You will need eight of each type. The inner scrolls are a simple C shape, but the ends could be thinned and spread to match the ends of the other scrolls (Fig. 14-3A). Be careful to shape each set of scrolls to match as closely as possible.

The large scrolls are shown with pieces welded on at the outer ends (Fig. 14-3B)

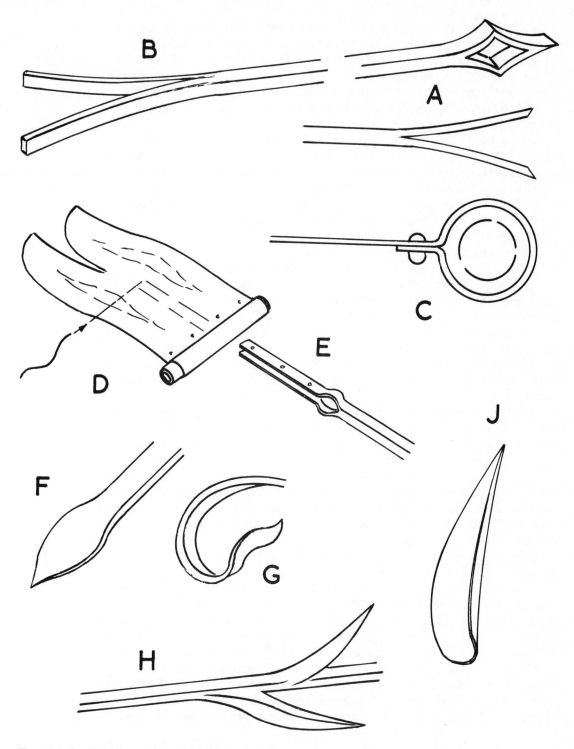

Fig. 14-4. Details of the wind vane rotating arm.

and where they meet the arm (Fig. 14-3C). Shape these ends to match. The inner ends could be finished in the same way, but they are shown with rosettes (Fig. 14-2C). These are discs with petal outlines, preferably hammered to a dished shape. They could be welded to the ends of the scrolls, but there is a risk of burning the thinner metal. It is better to roll the scroll end around a ¼-inch rod, which projects through holes in the rosettes and is rivetted (Fig. 14-3D). The rivet head then looks like the center of the flower.

Cut the letters from ³⁄₁₆- or ¼-inch plate. Make the N, S, and E letters 8 inches high and 5 inches wide, and the W slightly wider. Cut the arms to length and weld the letters to them.

Mark the positions of the arms on the pillar and weld these joints, being careful to finish with all the arms square to each other and to the pillar. Check the appearance of the assembly by viewing it from several directions before adding the scrolls. Adjustments are easier at this stage.

Join in the scrolls. They could be welded at each meeting. Some joints could be rivetted, bolted, or screwed. Small straps might be put around joints, either unaided or to supplement one of the other methods of joining. If the joints are not welded, it will be helpful to put jointing compound or paint between the parts before drawing them together, to reduce the risk of water being trapped and causing rust.

The vane (Fig. 14-2D) is formed around a tube that fits over the round top of the pillar. Make the tube to fit easily over the pillar and to contain a 1-inch steel ball, which forms the bearing in the same way as in Project 13. Weld on a plate to close the top of the tube and cut its length to come within about 1 inch of the collar on the pillar (Fig. 14-2E).

Split the end of the arm, so the two parts can be forged into an open arrow head with the meeting ends shaped to a fine point (Fig. 14-4A). At the tube, either split the arm or weld on two strips, ready to go around the tube and the sheet metal part (Fig. 14-4B). The sheet metal has to be formed into a two-pronged flag or pennant. As shown in Fig. 14-2F, this is 12 inches wide and 21 inches long. Use sheet steel ⅛ inch or slightly thinner. Allow for wrapping round the tube and rivetting (Fig. 14-4C). Cut to the outline, then hammer to a hollowed section (Fig. 14-4D). There could also be a slight curving in the length. Beside making the metal look more like a flag waving, the shaped sheet is stiffer than if it was left flat.

Shape the arm around the tube and along the flag, so you can put three ⅛-inch rivets through (Fig. 14-4E). Check squareness of the vane assembly so far.

Make two matching scrolls. They are shown with leaf decorations. Draw down the outer end and shape like a long leaf (Fig. 14-4F), then give it a twist as you shape it into the scroll (Fig. 14-4G). Along the arm of the scroll there are two leaves, either opposite each other or slightly staggered (Fig. 14-4H). Form each leaf from sheet metal, hollowed as well as curved in the length (Fig. 14-4J), then weld to the scroll arms.

If you want to add a badge or coat of arms, keep it symmetrical around the pivot of the vane, so it does not affect windage. Weld it above the top of the tube. Remove any rust from the steel and treat it with rust-inhibiting fluid, then paint in any colors you wish. Bed the pivot ball in thick grease and fit the vane tube over the pillar.

15

Exterior Lamp Bracket

In the days before electric lighting, exterior lights were oil or candle, and later coal gas. All of these required protection from the wind. Some of the lamps used for this purpose were very attractive. They supported glass screens and in turn were supported by pedestals or brackets. Today, with modern outside electric lighting, there is no need for protection from the wind, but casing or lanterns and brackets based on the earlier designs can add a touch of character to the outside lighting of your home. Some brackets could be copied for other uses, such as hanging signs or plant pots, but with a traditional lamp the effect is unusual and attractive.

This lamp and its bracket (Fig. 15-1) has a four-sided glassed casing with a sloping roof, in the style that was used for light sources with flames. The bracket is decorated with scrolls and the arm could be a square tube so the wires to the lamp are concealed. The back of the bracket is suitable for mounting on a post or against any type of wall.

The bracket is shown and described with snub end scrolls, which will exercise your skill and show your talents. If you want something simpler, you could make plain scrolls with the welded extra piece in the lower one. An electric lamp in a candle shape would be appropriate. Its holder is mounted on a tube, which conceals the wires.

Most of the parts of the lamp casing are fairly light section and involve some sheet metalwork, including soldering and brazing. Forged corner supports held with screws allow the lamp to be removed from the bracket if necessary.

The sheet metal roof would look attractive if made of copper or brass, which also have the advantage of being easy to solder. In any case the steel should be painted; if the top is not polished copper or brass it could be painted gold or a light color to contrast with the black of the other parts. Glass could be clear or tinted.

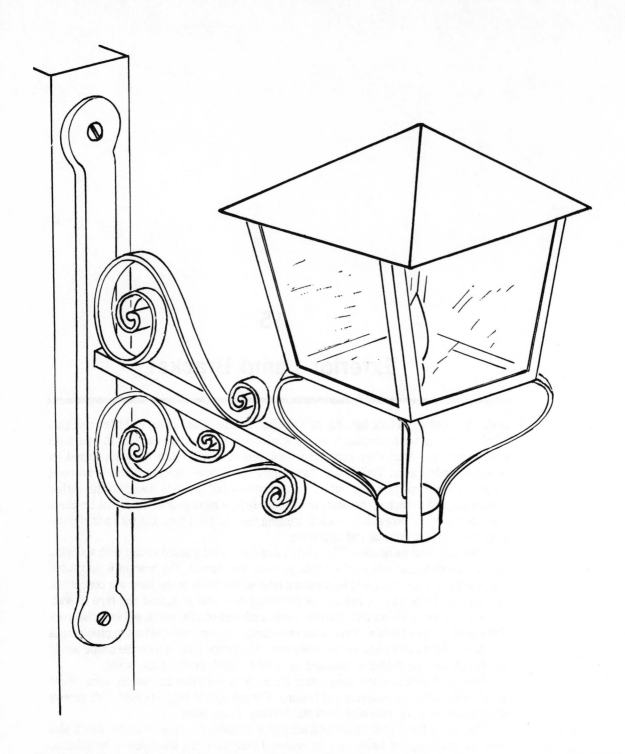

Fig. 15-1. A exterior lamp bracket based on an old design.

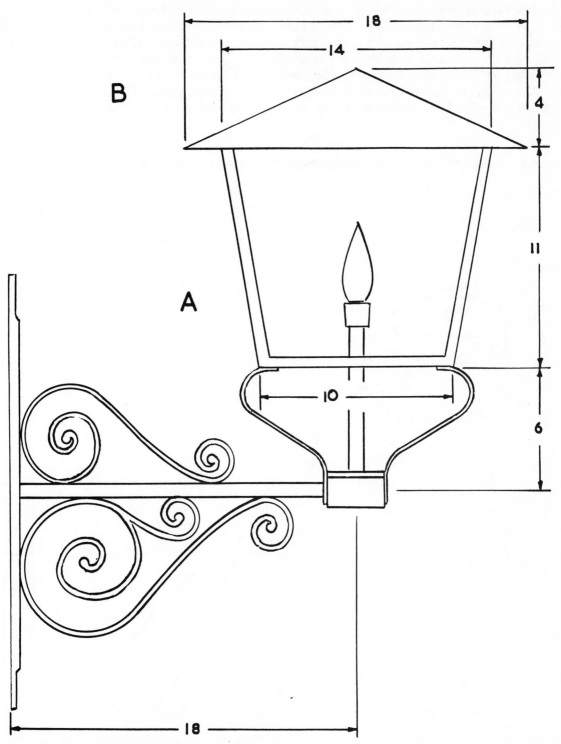

Fig. 15-2. Suggested sizes for the exterior lamp bracket.

Exact sizes are not critical, but sizes that give a good proportion are shown in Fig. 15-2. The back of the bracket may be ½-by-1½-inch strip and the arm ¾-inch square tube. Scroll parts are ¼-by-¾-inch section. Lamp supports are ¼ by ½ inch. Many of the lamp frame parts could be ½-by-½-inch angle only ¹⁄₁₆ inch or less thick, or sheet metal may be bent to suit. The roof could be sheet metal 16-gauge or less.

The connection between the bracket and the lamp is formed from a piece of 3-inch diameter tube (Fig. 15-3A) or a piece of strip wrapped round. The top is closed by a

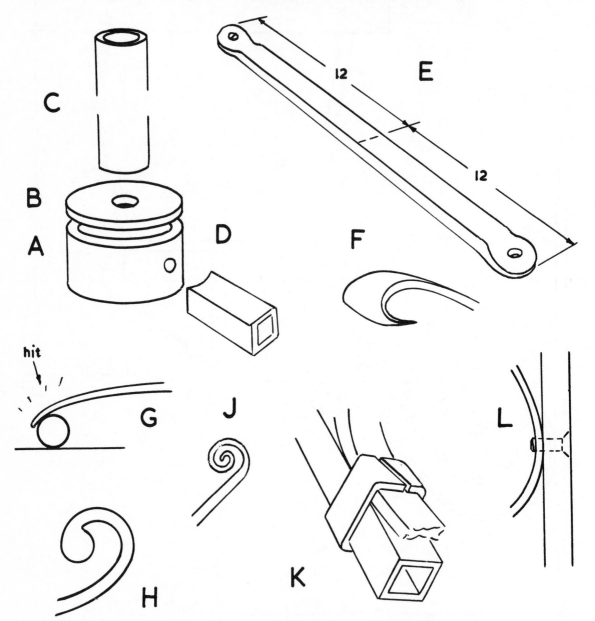

Fig. 15-3. Construction details of the bracket.

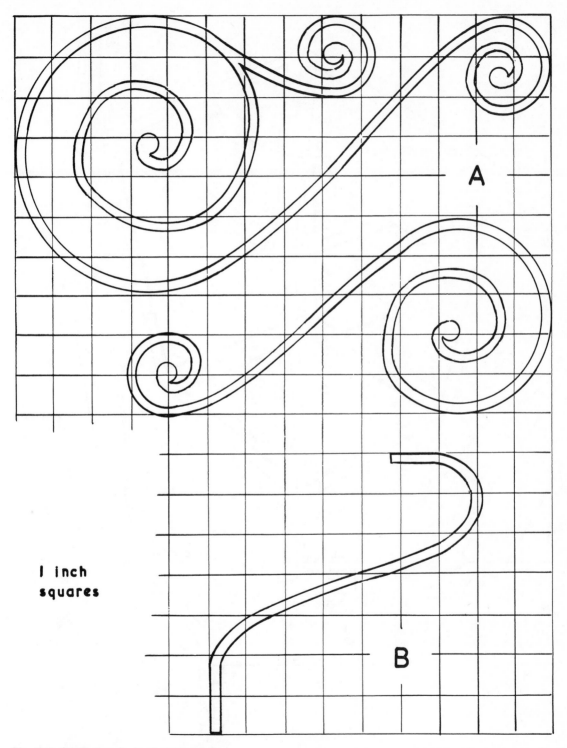

I inch
squares

A

B

Fig. 15-4. Scroll sizes for the lamp bracket.

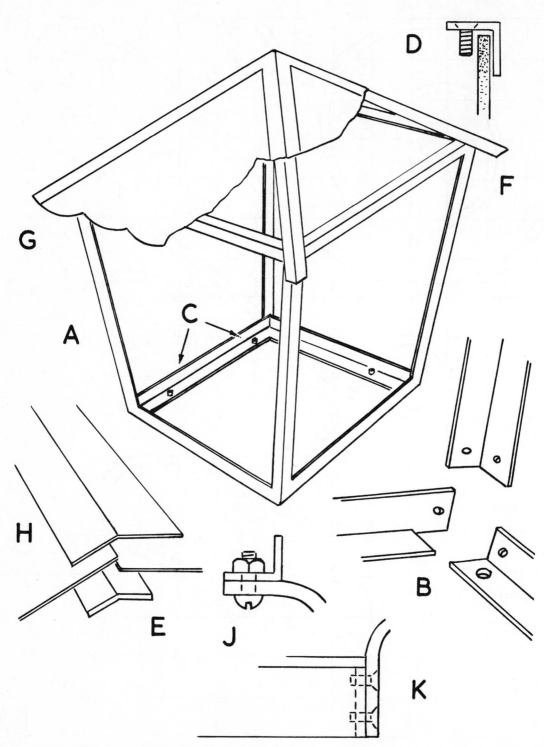

Fig. 15-5. Layout and construction of the lamp housing.

piece of sheet about ³⁄₁₆ inch thick brazed on (Fig. 15-3B). If these parts can be turned on a lathe, accuracy is easily obtained. The support for the lamp holder is 1-inch tube (Fig. 15-3C). Its length and the method of attaching the lamp holder will depend on available parts, but in the finished lamp the electric bulb should come about halfway up the glass height.

Braze or weld the lamp tube and the square arm tube to the junction part, with holes large enough to pass the electric wires (Fig. 15-3D). Leave the lamp tube too long, to be cut to length later.

Make the back bracket (Fig. 15-3E). Reduce and spread the ends to about half thickness, to take fixing screws or bolts. Weld the arm to the center around a hole to pass the electric wires. Check that the arm will be square to the wall in all directions.

Using the back and arm as a guide, set out the scrolls (Fig. 15-4A). For the simplest scrolls let the inner ends be merely cut off square. One alternative is to draw down and spread the ends, preferably with a moderately tight curl (Fig. 15-3F). For a snub end, draw the end down to about half thickness, then use a piece of rod and fire-weld the two together (Fig. 15-3G), so the inner curl of the scroll finishes in a knob (Fig. 15-3H). A similar appearance may be obtained by curling the drawn-down end tightly (Fig. 15-3J).

Fit the scrolls to the arm with collars (Fig. 15-3K), but use screws through the back (Fig. 15-3L) to make a strong assembly.

Prepare lengths of suitable angle for the lamp or lantern, or fold sheet about ¹⁄₁₆ inch thick. There are top and bottom square frames joined by corner uprights (Fig. 15-5A) to the overall sizes shown (Fig. 15-2A). Open the bottom and corner angles slightly and close in the top angles slightly, to allow for the conical shape.

At the bottom corners, cut the bottom pieces to fit into each other, with the uprights outside and rivetted to them (Fig. 15-5B). This allows holes to be drilled for ³⁄₁₆-inch bolts into the supporting brackets. The top corners could be the same or mitered.

To retain the glass in a way that allows you to replace it if it becomes broken, fit two countersunk screws in each horizontal piece (Fig. 15-5C and D).

The angle and sizes of parts of the roof are best found by measuring over the other parts after they have been assembled. Allow a good overhang (Fig. 15-2B). Make four corner pieces about ¹⁄₁₆ inch thick (Fig. 15-5E) to meet at the top and overhang at the corners sufficiently to support the roof panels (Fig. 15-5F). Solder or braze the meeting points at the apex. A rivet at each corner should be sufficient to hold to the frame.

Cut the roof panels to meet over the corner rafters. The edges may be left straight or cut to a pattern (Fig. 15-5G). Solder the panels to the rafters, then make cover strips to solder over the joints (Fig. 15-5H). Make sure the joint at the apex is closed, so rain cannot enter.

The supports that join the lantern to the round part on the bracket are diagonal to the square of the lantern. Shape them to the pattern (Fig. 15-4B). Use ³⁄₁₆-inch nuts and bolts into the lantern corners (Fig. 15-5J), but it will be neater to put two screws into each overlap at the lower joints (Fig. 15-5K).

Cut the glass for an easy fit in the framework. Rubber or plastic pads behind the retaining screws will prevent rattling. Attach the lamp holder to the tube and arrange the wiring. Make a trial assembly, then remove the lantern from the bracket and paint all surfaces, including those that will be inside and covered.

16

Domestic Hook Hardware

In earlier days the blacksmith made a large number of items for use around the home, particularly things for the kitchen, wash house, scullery, and outside buildings associated with farming. Many of these devices, mostly incorporating hooks, are useful today, although not always for their original purposes. If you furnish part of your home in country style, there are many things to make that will complement the wood furniture to create the right atmosphere. A number of the things our ancestors used indoors can be used on the patio, deck, or around a barbecue area. Some might be just decorative or be nostalgic reminders of earlier times, or they could have practical applications.

A smith can make many useful items from rod and bar of small section, so it is possible to get by using only a propane torch as a source of heat, if your equipment is limited. There is a large range of hooks to be made from round and square rod. You might not have a need for the basic meat hook (Fig. 16-1A), however, a hook could have one or both ends finished into knobs (Fig. 16-1B). If you use square rod, the center could be twisted and the ends drawn down round (Fig. 16-1C). One end could be a ring (Fig. 16-1D), either large for putting your fingers through or smaller to hang on a nail or another hook.

A long hook could have a ring or T handle for pulling a load (Fig. 16-1E). If you want to fit a wood handle, taking the end through and rivetting it (Fig. 16-1F) might be satisfactory, but a forged eye around the wood (Fig. 16-1G) will be stronger.

Similar hooks can be made with snub ends or tight scrolls (Fig. 16-1H) for hanging planters or similar things. They could be made with more open scrolls (Fig. 16-1J). A series of such hooks might be used as a chain and the number adjusted to suit the article hanging.

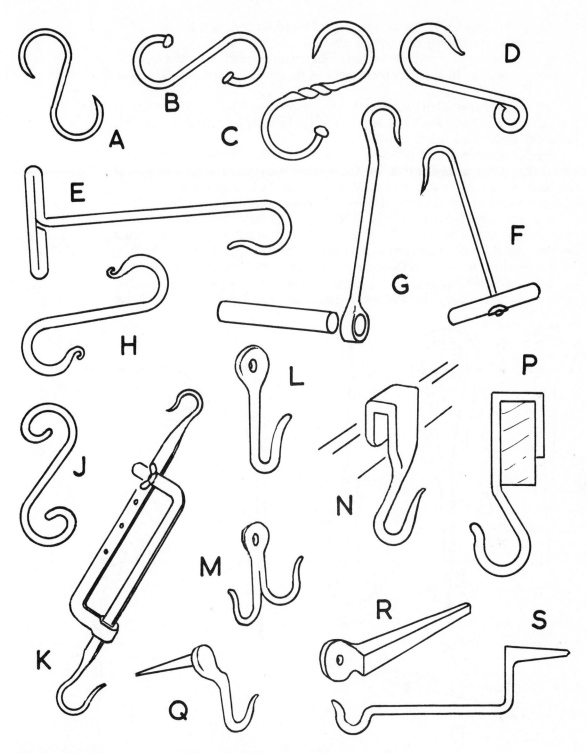

Fig. 16-1. Hooks in many forms can be made for use in the home.

An adjustable hook (Fig. 16-1K) was originally used for hanging a pot over a fire, but it would be another way of hanging a plant pot or flower display.

A hook to attach to a wall could be made with any pattern end, but with a flattened top for a screw (Fig. 16-1L). This could easily be developed into a double hook (Fig. 16-1M).

A hook might have a top to pass over and slide on a bar (Fig. 16-1N) or to go on a wood rail (Fig. 16-1P). For a tool or gun rack, hooks might be welded to a bar that has flattened ends to screw to a wall.

Another type of wall hook drives in. Ideally, the bend is thickened and squared for ease in driving with a hammer (Fig. 16-1Q). A variation on this has a flat palm instead of a hook for screwing to a piece of wood (Fig. 16-1R). Make a good squared top for hitting; the hammer will slip on a rounded end, which is more easily forged.

The various wall hooks do not have to be close to the wall. They may be extended from what was once a lantern bracket (Fig. 16-1S), to an item that will hold an electric lamp or a planter. Do not extend too far. Anything very large would be better as a bracket.

Steel skewers have uses in the kitchen or at a barbecue, and a gardener might be glad to have them when dealing with pot plants, marking rows, and planting seeds. They can be made in sizes from 8 to 18 inches. The basic skewer is tapered with a small ring

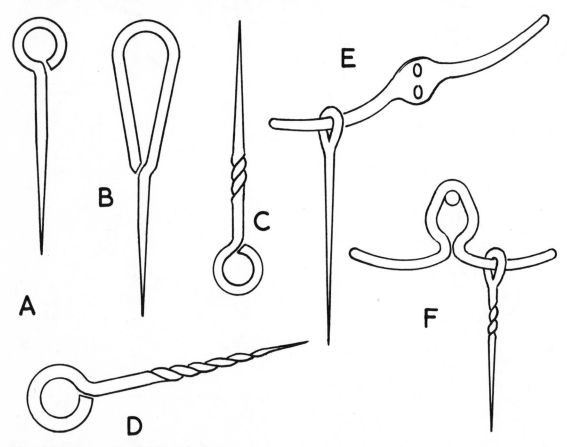

Fig. 16-2. Skewers are variations on hooks.

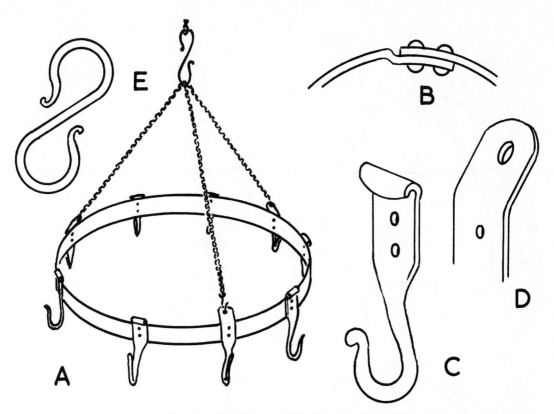

Fig. 16-3. A round arrangement of hooks, originally intended for drying herbs, might have other uses in a modern home.

top (Fig. 16-2A) or a bigger loop handle (Fig. 16-2B). If made of square bar it can be decorated with a twist (Fig. 16-2C), although if you draw down square it can be twisted almost to a point (Fig. 16-2D), which might be an advantage when dealing with some meat.

The simplest skewer rack is a two-way slender hook with a flattened center for screws (Fig. 16-2E). This could be elaborated into a looped rod (Fig. 16-2F). You can create your own ideas for a forged center.

A round rack suspended with a central hook was a common thing in early homes. It could have served as an herb rack, with herbs drying on hooks round the rim. It was sometimes called a Dutch crown, if it had looped top supports. A modern version might be used as a utensil rack over a central work area in a kitchen. It could also be used to hang tools for gardening or other purposes. It would take animal pelts or anything else that had to be dried.

A simple untensil rack (Fig. 16-3A) is based on a circle made from strip about ³⁄₁₆-by-1-inch section with a diameter about 18 inches. Overlap and rivet the ends (Fig. 16-3B). Make as many hooks as you require, with loops to suit your needs, probably with blunt or scroll ends (Fig. 16-3C). You could extend the tops as decorations. If necessary, make hooks of different sizes—possibly alternating large and small ones—to suit the items to be held.

Either drill the strip for hanging chains or make three hooks with extended tops

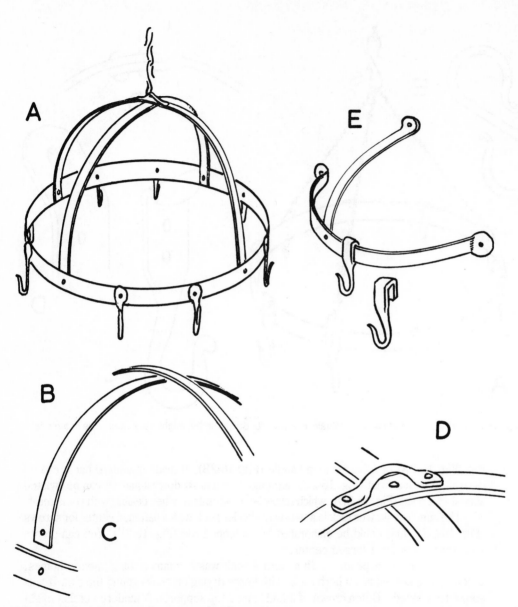

Fig. 16-4. This variation was known as a Dutch crown.

to take the chains (Fig. 16-3D). The suspending hook should be a fairly close S shape (Fig. 16-3E) to fit into a ring in the ceiling. Use light chain for suspension. Make hooks for connecting to the ring.

The Dutch crown (Fig. 16-4A) starts in a similar way. It uses a ring, but makes two crossing semi-circles of slightly lighter section strip (Fig. 16-4B) which overlaps at the top and is rivetted to the ring (Fig. 16-4C).

Space the hooks to suit. The first rack needed a spacing in multiples of three; this one is in multiples of four because of the different support arrangements. As in the other rack, make the hooks to suit your needs. In both cases flat or square stock allows you to decorate with twists.

Overlap at the top and rivet through, then attach a loop to one piece (Fig. 16-4D). You could join together several hooks instead of using a chain.

If you do not have a kitchen arrangement that would allow a central rack to hang, you could make half a Dutch crown to attach to a wall (Fig. 16-4E). Flatten the loop ends to take screws and arrange as many hooks as you wish. Instead of rivetting you could arrange the hooks to slide on the rail.

A circular rack is suitable for a central light. The light and its shade could be suspended over the work area, with the utensils hanging within reach all round it.

Rust protection should be provided. Warm, moist air rises and would attack untreated steel. Apply several coats of paint, preferably over a coat of rust-inhibiting fluid.

17

Fireplace Smithing

The days when an open fire was essential in every home have passed, but there has been a resurgence of interest in open fireplaces. Flaming logs make a focal point in a room, particularly if the equipment in and around the fireplace has a traditional country appearance to create a nostalgic and workmanlike atmosphere that is lacking in many modern homes.

Because much of the equipment used where wood or coal was burned had been made by the local blacksmith and was not mass-produced, there are any examples from which a modern smith can make attractive reproductions. Project 10 shows pokers with a variety of handles, and other equipment could be made using a similar design.

Within a fireplace large enough to take whole logs, the supports for the wood are a pair of andirons, sometimes called firedogs. Basically, each of the two andirons has a strong bar, supported on divided legs at the front and one or two upright legs behind (Fig. 17-1A). There might be an upright part at the back (Fig. 17-1B), but the place for decoration is at the high front (Fig. 17-1C).

Because the material becomes hot, do not be tempted to forge very fine decoration that would warp or burn on the front. The size of available space will govern the steel used, but anything less than ¾ inch square is inadvisable. A clearance of 4 inches should be enough for ash to fall down to be raked out. A simple front is a curled end over bent feet (Fig. 17-1D), to give a token animal appearance. Legs may be spread and curved (Fig. 17-1E). A twist and a heart might go above that (Fig. 17-1F). A scroll front could have scroll legs (Fig. 17-1G). Many old andirons included a smith's twisted cage (Fig. 17-1H). An addition could be a hook or hole on the upright to hold a bar across, which prevents wood from falling forward (Fig. 17-1J).

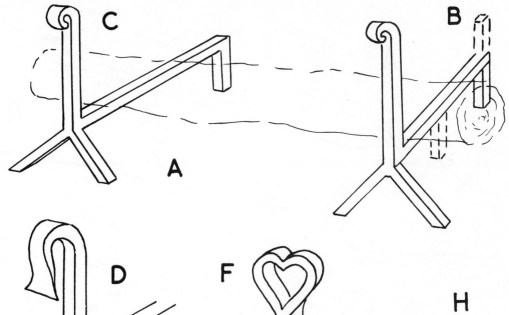

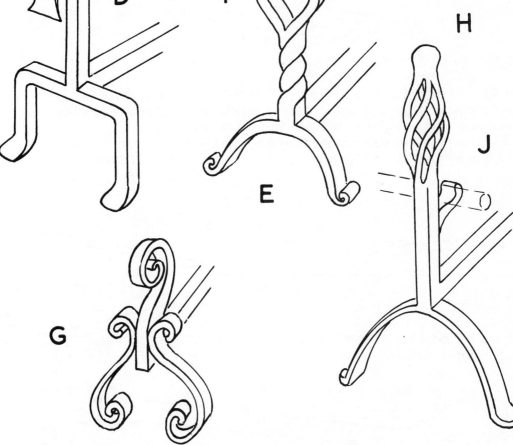

Fig. 17-1. Andirons for use in a fireplace offer the blacksmith an opportunity for decoration.

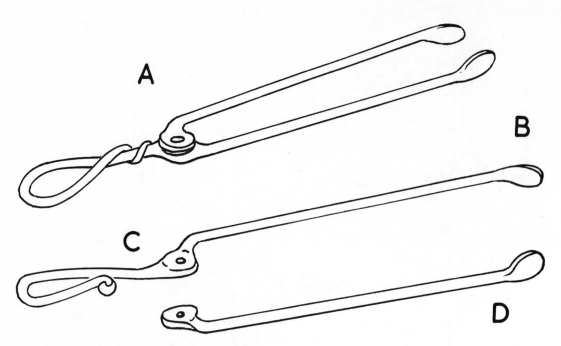

Fig. 17-2. One type of fire tongs that can be made.

Smaller and lighter andirons were used in front of the fire so tongs, shovel, poker, and any other tools could rest on them ready to be picked up. They could be based on ½-inch square bar with a design to match the andirons in the fireplace.

Much of the manipulating of a fire can be done with a poker and a rake, but when something hot has to be picked up you need tongs. The first type (Fig. 17-2A) requires

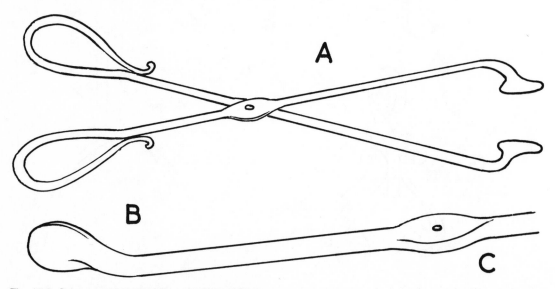

Fig. 17-3. Scissors-type tongs are an alternative form.

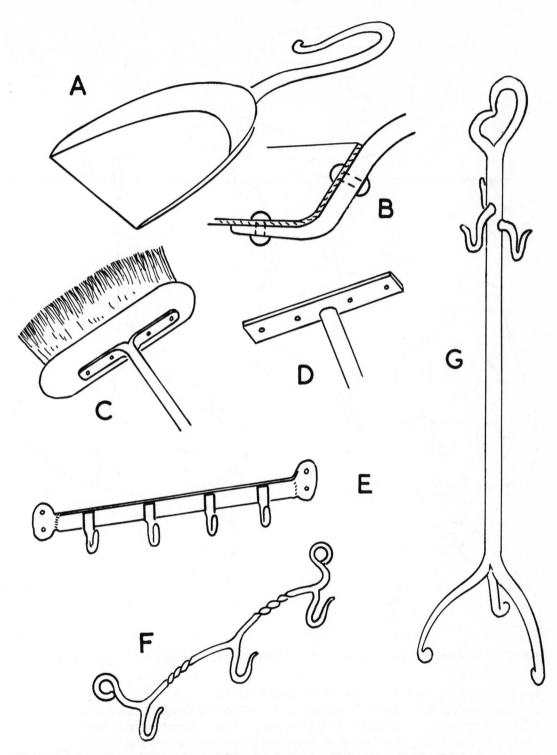

Fig. 17-4. Among other tools to make are a shovel and a brush, with hanging racks for all tools.

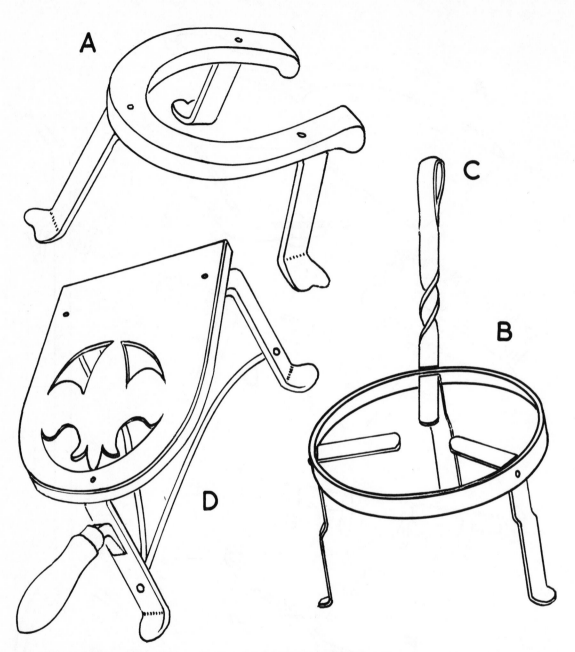

Fig. 17-5. A trivet for use by a fire may be based on a horseshoe, be made round, or have decorated sheet metal top.

two hands, but the capacity is ample for anything in the fire.

Make one half of the tongs with a simple loop handle or any design to match your poker—⅜- or ½-inch rod is suitable. Upset the end so there is enough metal to forge a large palm (Fig. 17-2B). Shape below the handle and flatten to take a rivet (Fig. 17-2C). Form the other half to match, but without a handle (Fig. 17-2D). Drill for the rivet and put in a temporary bolt, so you can experiment with the action and alter curves if necessary. Loosely rivet parts together, but there should not be so much play that the joint wobbles. You could put pieces of shimstock between the parts as you rivet, then pull them out.

A type that operates on the scissors principle, might still need two hands, unless the required opening is small (Fig. 17-3A). Round rod ⅜-inch diameter will make comfortable handles on tongs about 20 inches long. The two parts are the same. Decorate the loop handles in any way you wish. Forge palms on the bent ends (Fig. 17-3B). Flatten for the pivot rivet at about the center (Fig. 17-3C). Moving the pivot towards the palms gives more leverage, but increased handle movement. Moving the other way increases capacity, but means more pressure on the handles. As with the other tongs, use a temporary pivot and try the action before rivetting.

A shovel and brush are needed to keep the hearth clean. If you place a pair of andirons in front of the fire, they could have long handles to rest there. Otherwise they may have short handles with loops for hanging.

In both cases you can regard the tools as pokers with different ends, so any of the poker design handles can be used—so long as they will hang, if that is what is needed. Make a shovel blade from sheet steel about 12 gauge (Fig. 17-4A). Taper the sides but keep a fairly high back, so the handle can take rivets both ways (Fig. 17-4B).

The brush should be about 9 inches across, preferably made of soft bristles or hairs. Split and open the handle end for screws into the wood (Fig. 17-4C) or weld on a flat piece (Fig. 17-4D).

A wall rack for hearth tools can have hooks on a rail (Fig. 17-4E). There could be some shaping and twisting (Fig. 17-4F). An alternative is a stand (Fig. 17-4G). These traditionally have three feet, so as to stand firm on an uneven hearth. Make the stand with a matching handle and enough hooks to take the tools.

Another three-legged item for the hearth is a trivet. The prefix ''tri'' means three. Its purpose was to act as a stand for a kettle pulled off the fire or stood there to get warm. One popular traditional trivet is made from a horseshoe (Fig. 17-5A). Rivet the three legs through nail holes. Make sure the top is flat. A simple round trivet may have the tops of the legs bent in to provide extra support (Fig. 17-5B). A trivet close to a fire might get hot, so an extended handle should be provided (Fig 17-5C).

Trivets were often given sheet metal tops decorated with piercing. A long D shape puts the flat end towards the fire and there can be a wood handle at the other side (Fig. 17-5D). Braces between the legs provide rigidity.

18

Boot Aids

Anyone who wears boots in muddy conditions will welcome two aids that a blacksmith can make. One is a scraper to remove mud and the other helps pull off the boots. A scraper just above ground level outside the door may be simple or ornate. One form of boot remover is something called a cricket: there are jaws into which you put the heel of the boot, while the other foot holds down the device as you haul your foot out of the gripped boot.

The essential part of a boot scraper is a vertical blade to draw the boot over. This could be a piece of ¼-by-1½-inch bar 6 inches long (Fig. 18-1A), supported between two uprights (Fig. 18-1B). Shoulder the scraper ends to go through punched holes in the uprights (Fig. 18-1C) and rivet over on the outside. The uprights can drive into the ground or be set in concrete. One leg may be bent to go into a wall (Fig. 18-1D). There is scope for decoration of the uprights. You could turn over the top to a snub end (Fig. 18-1E) or a more open scroll (Fig. 18-1F). The tops might be split and formed into a heart or other motif (Fig. 18-1G). If you need to steady yourself while you scrape each boot, one upright might be high enough to provide a hand grip (Fig. 18-1H).

You might not remove as much mud as you wish on this scraper, so a hand scraper could also be made. The handle end is any pattern you wish, but draw down the other end to a thin broad edge (Fig. 18-1J). Finish it with rounded edges so there is no risk of scratching the boot.

A boot scraper is usually arranged beside a door and square to the wall, so a more elaborate form could be on the wall to provide rigidity (Fig. 18-1K). The arched outer piece can have a spike to go into the ground or a foot for screwing down. Its top can be anything from a flat rivetted palm to a shaped extension.

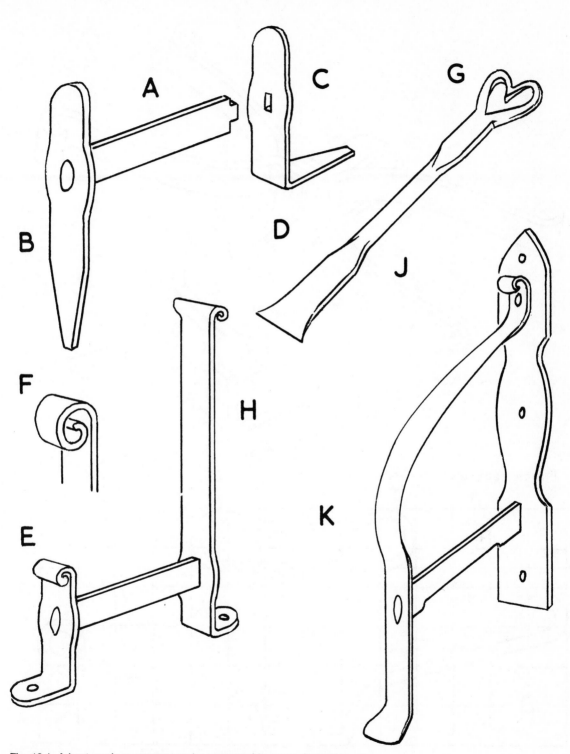

Fig. 18-1. A boot or shoe scraper can be supported in many decorative ways.

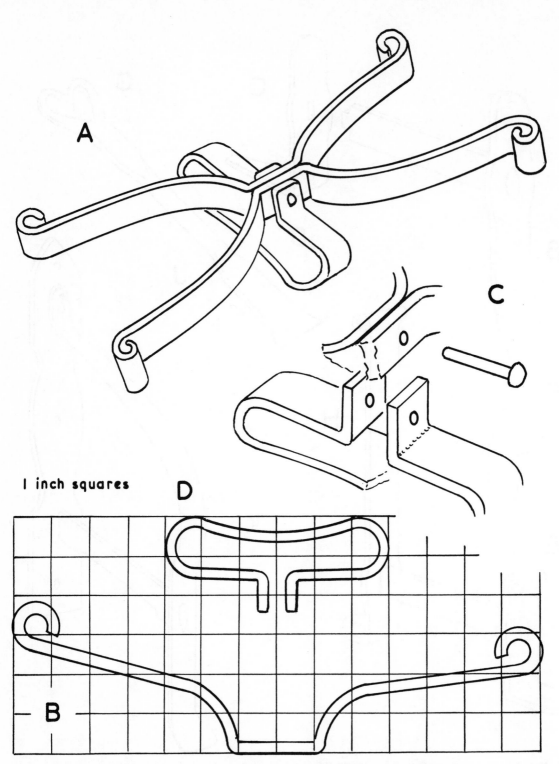

A

C

I inch squares

D

B

Fig. 18-2. This aid to boot or shoe removal can be reversed to suit different sizes of footwear.

The boot remover (Fig. 18-2A) is double-ended so boots of widely different sizes can be fitted. You could use ¼-by-¾-inch strip. The ends may be simply flared, but they are shown with moderately scrolled ends. Make two parts of the pattern (Fig. 18-2B). Their flat centers meet and are held with a rivet that also goes through the foot, on which the assembly rocks (Fig. 18-2C).

Make the foot to its pattern (Fig. 18-2D). The hollow in the bottom is to prevent sideways rocking if the ground is uneven. A tight rivet alone should be sufficient to hold the parts, but you could also weld or braze them together. Remove any rough edges from the parts that will be in contact with a boot. A burnt oil treatment would be satisfactory if you do not want to use a painted finish.

19

Coat and Umbrella Stand

A steel stand for hanging coats and hats has advantages of being more rigid and stable than a similar wood piece of furniture. This stand includes rings for umbrellas, canes, or any long thin items, such as bats or golf clubs (Fig. 19-1). Comparatively light and easily worked rods are used. Strength and stiffness comes from the ropelike twisted construction.

Sections depend on how heavy you want the stand to be and the equipment you have to provide sufficient heat when making the twists. However, ½-inch round rod, with ¼-by-¾-inch flat strip for the rings should make a satisfactory stand. The suggested overall sizes (Fig. 19-2A) may be modified. If you increase the height, also increase the spread of the feet for stability.

Start by making the rings, which should be about 6 inches diameter. Each could be made continuous by welding the strip ends together, but the ends may be flattened and spread so a rivet can be used (Fig. 19-2B). If the palms are neatly rounded they could be regarded as decoration. At each level the three rings meet and have the inner parts taken in so the rods through them do not have to spread very much (Fig. 19-2C). Shape each set of rings to give compact junctions at the center of the rope, then rivet them together (Fig. 19-2D). Make the second set to match the first.

When the rods are twisted together to make the pillar, the effect is an overall shortening. How much the shortening will be depends on the tightness of the twist: a steeply angled twist uses up less length than one that has more turns in a given length. Consequently, it is difficult to estimate what length to cut the rods. It is advisable to allow at least 6 inches more than the final length anticipated, then work from the bottom up and shape the coat hooks after the other parts are finished. You will need an assistant

Fig. 19-1. A coat and umbrella stand made with twisted rods.

to steady the long assembly at this point, which will help you achieve a symmetrical top.

For the feet, flatten a palm on each rod (Fig. 19-2E). Fold it under (Fig. 19-2F), then adjust it to rest flat on the floor later, so the assembly will stand upright. Bend the legs to shape (Fig. 19-3A) and twist the rods together just enough to hold them, spread at 120° to each other (Fig. 19-2G).

Heat the rods and introduce the lower assembly of three rings to come between

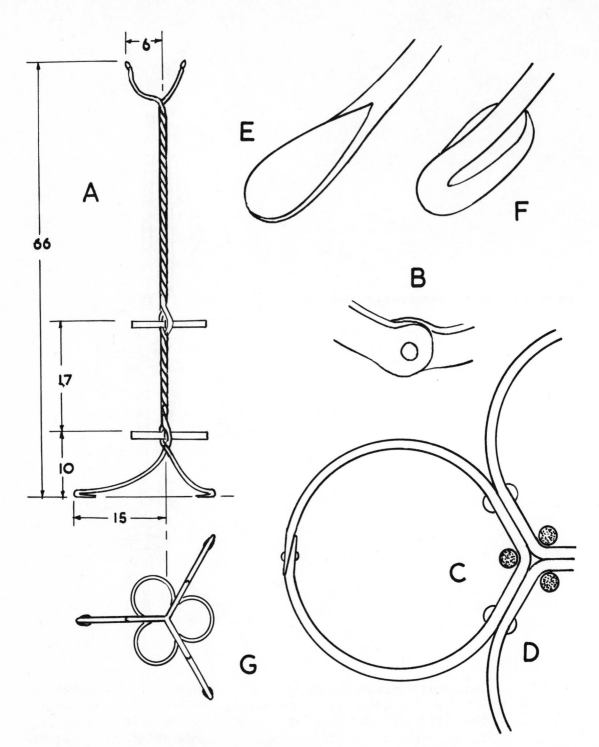

Fig. 19-2. Sizes and details of the coat and umbrella stand.

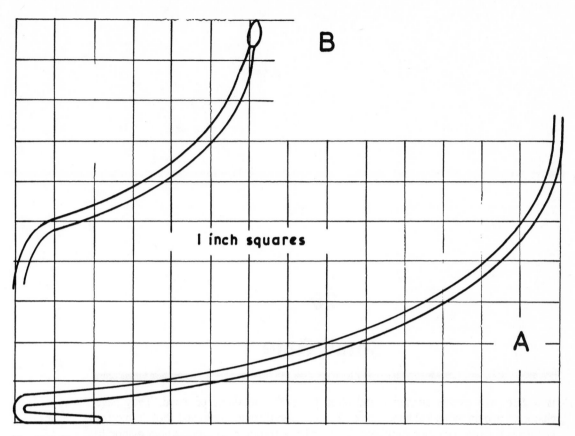

Fig. 19-3. Shapes to bend parts of the stand.

the spread feet. Continue twisting above the rings, closing onto them as tightly as possible. Further heating may be done in a fire, but it is helpful to have a propane torch to maintain heat where you need it and to compensate for any uneven heat. Holding the parts already twisted in a vise while further twisting is done allows you to work along progressively. If the parts yet to be twisted are kept spread, you can level them around.

When sufficient lower twisted work has been done, bring in the upper group of three rings in a similar way directly above the others, then continue twisting above until there is sufficient length. Try to keep the pillar straight as you twist. Minor errors can be hammered out later, but attempting to straighten a bad kink will affect the appearance of the twist at that point.

The three rods will probably not finish with extensions of the same length; trim them if necessary. Treatment of the ends can vary. There could be small scrolls or snub ends, but if you want to slip coat loops over them it would be better not to enlarge them. One treatment would be to draw down to finish with round or elliptical knobs no bigger in diameter than the rod (Fig. 19-3B).

Check that the parts at top and bottom are evenly spaced, the pillar stands upright, and the rings are level. View the stand from several directions before finishing with paint.

20

Small Gate

Iron gates are always attractive and often preferable to those of wood. They have character and an individual appearance. You can see through them and they frame the picture of a garden or other view behind. Some large traditional gates are very elaborate and fine examples of the blacksmith craft. A simpler gate can be quite effective in modern surroundings and is more suitable for making with lesser skill and limited equipment.

The gate in Fig. 20-1 is suitable for closing a gap in a fence of any type, whether wood, stone, or metal. As shown, it is just above waist height and suitable for an opening about 30 inches wide. The same methods could be used for gates of other sizes. The width has to be divisible by eight.

In Fig. 20-2A the gate centers are 3½ inches. If you want to keep out most dogs and other animals of similar size the centers should not be more than 4 inches.

Several types of hinges and latches could be used, but the instructions here include pintle hinges and a simple latch—which can also be made, so the whole gate will be your own work.

Most flat parts may be ¼-by-1¼-inch strip and the rods may be ½-inch diameter. There is not much shaping to be done, but you need equipment for punching square holes and be able to drill holes up to ½-inch diameter. If the gate is to be completed in the traditional way there is no need for welding, but if you have welding equipment, it could be used to strengthen some joints.

It will be helpful to lay out the main lines fullsize, so you can fit parts over the outline to get the assembly square. It is also possible to make the individual parts and square them during a temporary assembly to obtain the details of the diagonal brace, which is the only piece that has to be marked from a layout or a temporary assembly.

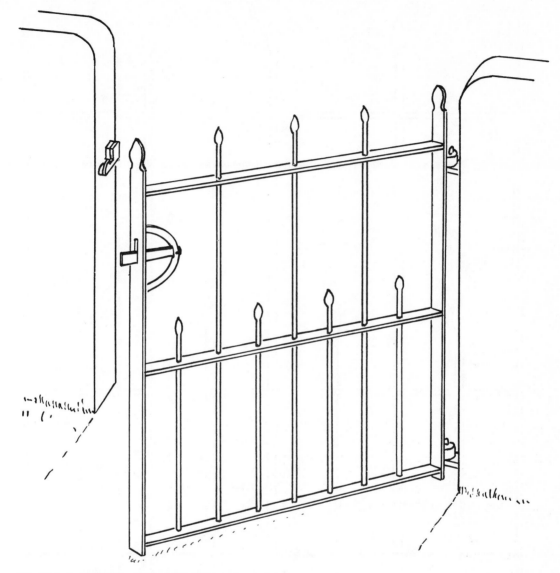

Fig. 20-1. A small gate made of flat strips and round rods.

Mark out the two sides with the positions of other parts. One will have the latch (Fig. 20-3A) and the other the hinges (Fig. 20-3B). Mark out the three rails (Fig. 20-3C). Cut tenons on the ends and punch holes for them in the sides (Fig. 20-3D). The widening of the strip that will result might be regarded as decoration and evidence of traditional methods, but you could also file the edges straight. Make the tenons long enough for rivetting outside later.

Make the rods. Shoulder their lower ends to fit into holes in the bottom rail (Fig. 20-3E) and long enough to allow for rivetting. They need not be reduced much: ⅜ inch would be satisfactory. The upper ends could be simply rounded. They might be drawn

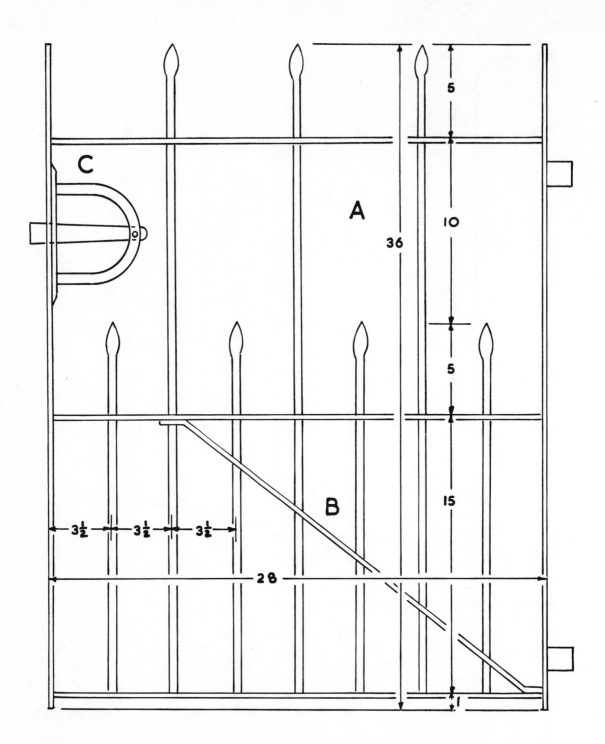

Fig. 20-2. Suggested sizes for the small gate.

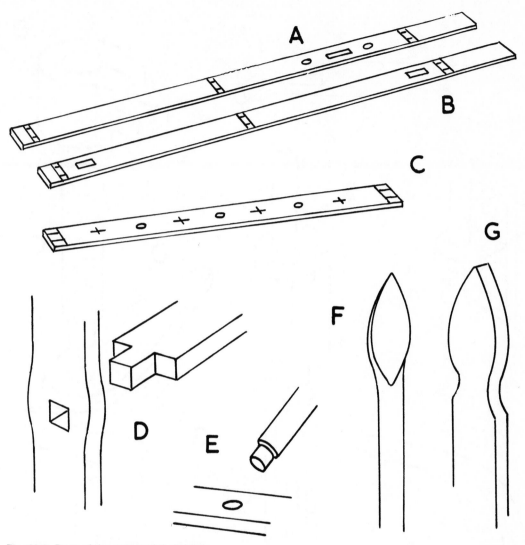

Fig. 20-3. Parts of the gate and their joints.

down and formed into twists or scrolls; here they are shown made into spears or leaves. The spear is a simple shaping (Fig. 20-3F). A leaf could be made from it by giving it a wavy section. Make all the ends to match, but slight variations can be regarded as an indication of hand work. Shape the tops of the sides to match (Fig. 20-3G).

Drill the top two rails so the rods will slide through fairly tightly. Drill the bottom rail to suit the shouldered rod ends. From your layout or a temporary assembly, mark out the diagonal brace (Fig. 20-2B). Drill for a rivet into the bottom rail. The upper end fits around a rod. The brace will have to take any downward load that would distort the gate and make it fall out of square. Be careful that the gate is not made with a built-in sag. It is wiser to assume that it will drop a little during its first use and to make it so it is a degree or so more than square at the hinged side. You might be able to drill

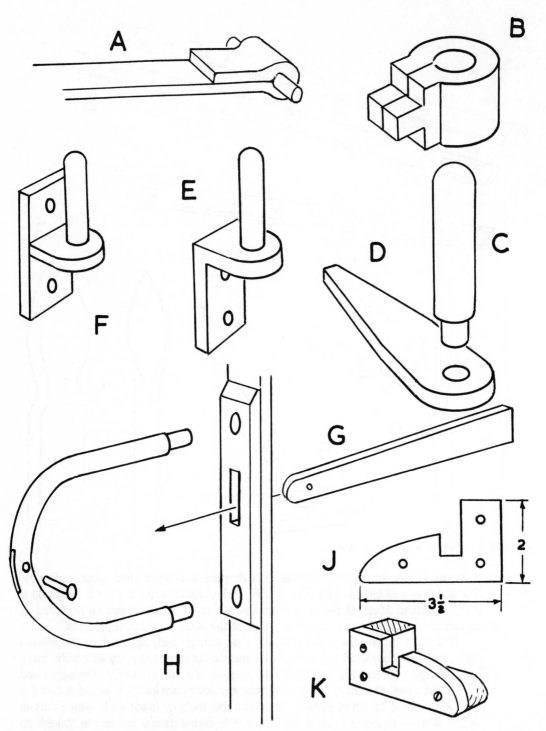

Fig. 20-4. Details of the gate latch and hinges.

104

intermediate rod holes diagonally, but will probably have to make final adjustments to fit the rods with a round file.

The gate can be made to lift off its hinges, with ½-inch rod used for the pintles. Other parts may be made from the same size strip as the gate. Wrap a strip around a short piece of rod (Fig. 20-4A). If the rod is about 9/16 inch, this will ensure clearance on the ½-inch pintles. Make two of these loops and cut tenons on them to fit punched holes in the gate side (Fig. 20-4B). Rivet them in place.

Make the pintles from ½-inch rod shouldered to fit holes in supporting strips (Fig. 20-4C). Round the tops of the pintles. It is easier to hang the gate after lifting off if the lower pintle is made longer than the upper one, so you do not have to position both hinges at the same time—2½ inches at the top and 3½ inches at the bottom would be suitable. If the supports can be driven into the gate post, they may be pointed (Fig. 20-4D). If they have to be screwed they may be bent (Fig. 20-4E) or rivetted to back pieces (Fig. 20-4F).

The latch is shown with a stiffening strip on the side (Fig. 20-2C). This is optional; you might consider the side stiff enough. The latch is ¼-inch strip, which could be parallel, but it looks better if tapered from 1 inch to about ¾ inch. Drill it for a ¼-inch rivet (Fig. 20-4G).

Make a slot in the ½-inch rod for the latch bar end before bending it. The loop may be 5 inches across. Shoulder the ends to go through the side and the stiffening strip for rivetting (Fig. 20-4H). Make the slot in the side so the latch bar will drop to just below horizontal and lift about 1 inch.

The catchplate lets the latch bar slide up and drop into a notch when the gate is slammed (Fig. 20-4J). It also acts as a gate stop. How it is mounted depends on the type of gate post, but screws through a wood packing, to give clearance, will suit many positions (Fig. 20-4K).

Attach the latch parts to their sides and check the action. Fit the tenons on the rails into their holes in the sides. Draw the parts tightly together as you rivet them. Rivet the diagonal brace to the bottom rail and temporarily clamp its upper end to the center rail. Check that the overall shape is correct and that there is no twist in the assembly. Put in the rods and rivet them through the bottom rail, checking frequently as you progress that the overall shape is maintained.

Use the gate to mark positions of the pintles and the catchplate on the gate posts. Allow adequate ground clearance and see that both pintle brackets share the support to avoid undue wear on one of them. When you paint, pay particular attention to undersides and inside angles, to reduce the risk of rust.

21

Scrolled Gate

Scrolls can form an attractive infill for a gate. Many old gates have scrolls as their main theme, often in many sizes and with elaborations of leaves and other decorations. In a modern setting a simpler arrangement is usually more appropriate. A large range of designs are possible, but this example (Fig. 21-1) uses a large number of identical scrolls, with a panel of twisted bars at the center.

This is a high gate, but the same design could be adapted to form a single lower gate or a pair of drive gates. The suggested overall size is 36 inches wide and 48 inches high over the frame. However, you might need a different size to fit an existing opening, or if you already have scroll irons or other shaping devices, the sizes could be adjusted to suit them.

The sides and rails may be ¼-by-1¼-inch strip. The uprights are ½-inch square bars. The scrolls should also be ½ inch wide, but the thickness could be ³⁄₁₆ or ¼ inch. Frame assembly is very similar to that of the small gate. Pintle hinges could be used, but a different method of fastening is suggested. Scrolls are best attached by welding.

The scrolls have to fit against each other within the framework, so it is advisable to make at least one or two scrolls first to check sizes (Fig. 21-2A). In the fairly light section it is possible to alter sizes by springing, but it would be unwise to alter the shapes very much.

The gate sides are the same, except that there are hinges on one (Fig. 21-2B). Make and fit hinge loops as on the small gate. Top and center rails are almost the same (Fig. 21-2C) and the bottom rail is the same, but without all the holes. The ends of the uprights may be shouldered to fit holes (Fig. 21-2D), but the long bars should go through punched square holes in the center rail (Fig. 21-2E). Prepare tenon joints between the rails and

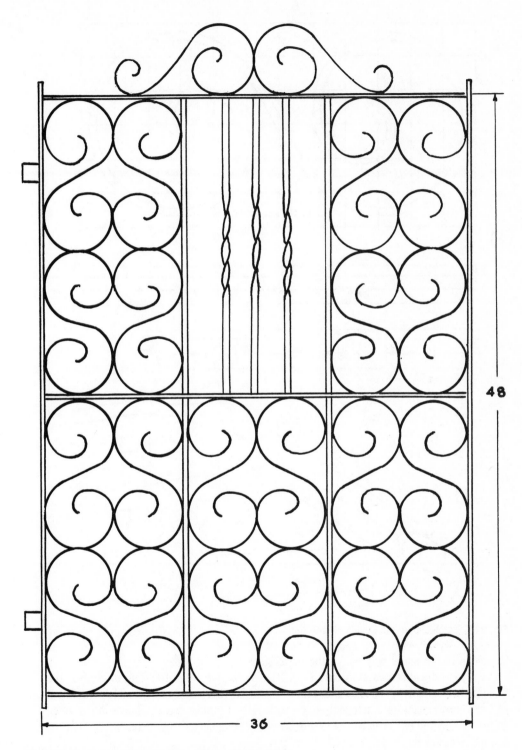

Fig. 21-1. A gate decorated with scrolls and twisted bars.

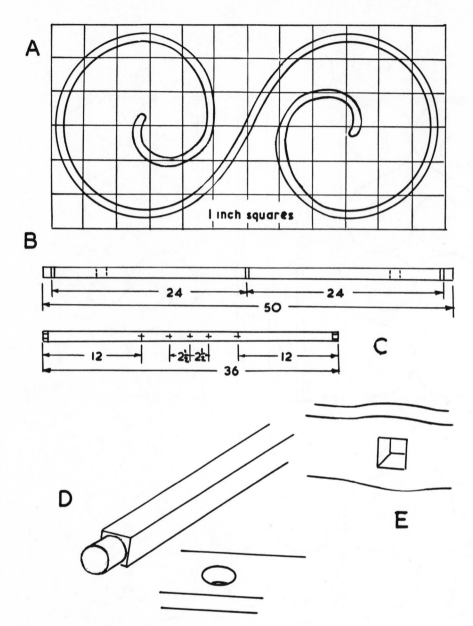

A

1 inch squares

B

24   50   24

12   2¹⁄₄ 2¹⁄₄   12
36

C

D

E

Fig. 21-2. Scroll shape and details of gate parts.

the sides in the same way as for the small gate.

Prepare the three twisted bars (Fig. 21-3A). Leave them too long until after the twisting has been done, so allowance can be made for shortening and possible adjustment of twist positions. Use a side as a guide to length. Countersink the holes in the rails, so the shouldered ends can be rivetted flush—projecting heads might interfere with fitting the scrolls closely.

Assemble the framework, including the uprights. Check squareness by comparing

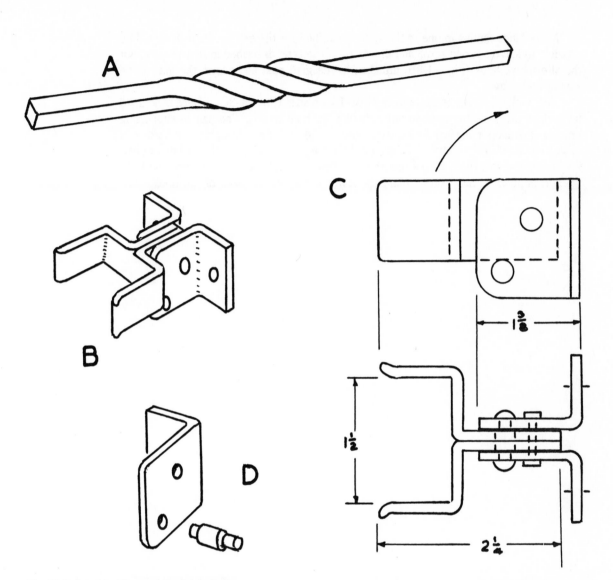

Fig. 21-3. A twisted bar and the latch design.

diagonal measurement, and see that the assembly is without twist. As with the small gate, beware of a built-in sag. It is better to have a very slight rise from the hinge side, to allow for possible settling in use.

Make 20 matching scrolls. Test them in place and make any slight adjustments necessary. Weld them in position, to the parts of the frame they touch and to each other. If you want to follow tradition you could use rivets or collars instead of welds. For a modern gate, however, welding is more appropriate and bonds the whole assembly, so there is no risk of movement between the parts later.

The two scrolls on top of the gate are made the same as the others, except only partial turns are made for the outer ends. Check that they match each other. Weld them together and to the top rail.

Make hinge pintles in one of the ways described for the smaller gate. It would be possible to leave out one scroll and fit a latch of the type described in that project, but the alternative hook (Fig. 21-3B) attaches to the gate post and allows the gate to be swung both ways.

The hook latch may be made from ⅛-by-1-inch strip (Fig. 21-3C). There is no need for a close fit. Bend the hook to have about ¼-inch clearance. The pair of supporting brackets are deeper and include a stop to prevent the hook from dropping past horizontal (Fig. 21-3D). This is a short shouldered rod rivetted in position. A bolt is a better pivot for the hook than a rivet. Check that there is clearance between the stop and the hook when it is lifted. If necessary, round the lower corner of the back of the hook.

22

Fences and Railings

Smith-made fences and railings make attractive alternatives to wood, stone, brick, or other types of barriers or border markers of your property. They could match gates or be independent pieces of useful decoration. A fence could be full-depth or it might be arranged on top of a wood or masonry wall. Suggestions for both types are given in this project. The range of possible designs is almost unlimited, but those shown will give you ideas to develop to suit your own requirements (Figs. 22-1 and 22-2).

The decorative parts of a full-depth steel fence have to be supported. It is generally unsatisfactory to try to build in supports as parts of the design. The simplest arrangement is a series of wood posts, to which the steelwork is screwed (Fig. 22-3A). Concrete posts could be used in a similar way. Steel posts of various sections are possible. Round tubes do not permit very neat joints. If you can get square tubing (Fig. 22-3B), screws could be tapped into it. T- and L-section stakes might have the fence sections bolted through (Fig. 22-3C). A post with this section does not have a very good resistance to being pushed over. Its foot could be bedded in concrete, and a soil plate (Fig. 22-3D) rivetted on will also increase its resistance to movement.

The spacing of posts and the lengths of bays of steelwork will have to be arranged to suit your needs, but in most circumstances it is unwise to make the distance between posts more than 72 inches. The example drawn (Fig. 22-1A) is 48 inches long and 27 inches between top and bottom rails. If you are building up a pattern you must choose a length that allows symmetrical spacing. If you want to keep out most animals, no space should be more than 4 inches.

Rails may be joined to the ends with tenon joints (Fig. 22-3E), in a similar way to the gates. Rail ends could be turned up or down and rivetted (Fig. 22-3F). It is possible

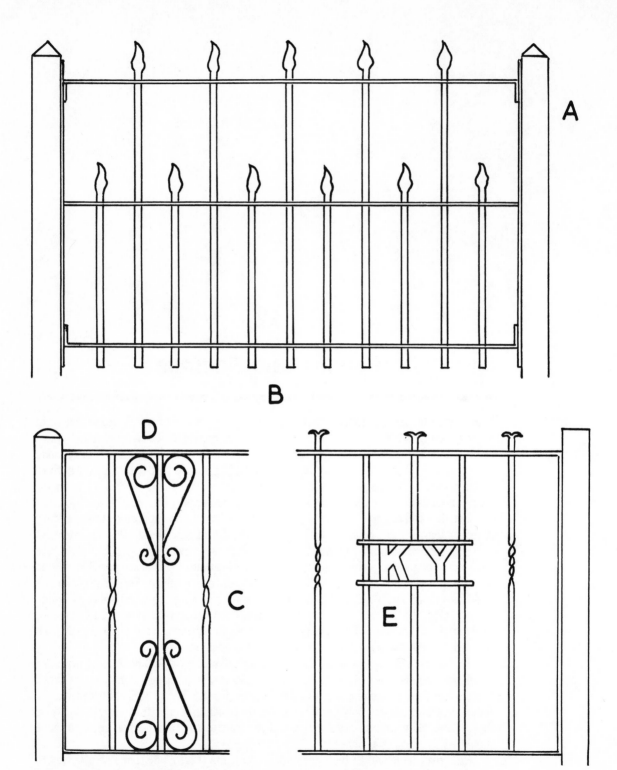

Fig. 22-1. Railings can be made with spiked rods or scrolls, or incorporate initials or badges.

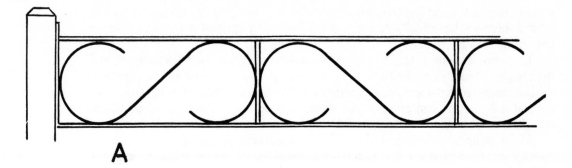

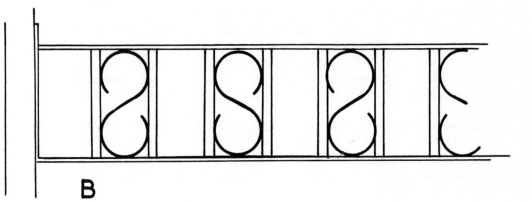

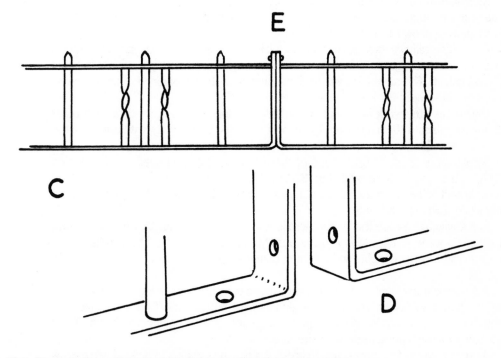

Fig. 22-2. These shallow railings are intended to go along the top of a wall fence.

to make the top rail and ends continuous (Fig. 22-3G), but if you do this at the bottom as well there will be difficulty in lining up rail holes, and uprights out of true become very obvious to a viewer.

In the first example (Fig. 22-1A), the rails and ends may be ¼-by-1¼-inch strip and the uprights ½-inch diameter rods. The uprights can be shouldered and rivetted into the bottom rail, as in the small gate, but they could be taken through (Fig. 22-1B). Mark out and drill the rails and prepare their ends for attaching to the fence ends. Check straightness. The rails must finish straight and horizontal if the fence is to look correct.

Make the uprights with spear (Fig. 22-3H), or leaf (Fig. 22-3J) tops. Drill the fence ends for screws to the posts. A ⅜-inch coach screw at top and bottom should be sufficient for wood posts. Use similar size bolts for metal. Assemble the complete bay of fencing, checking squareness and lack of twist as you weld the uprights in place.

If you use square bars for uprights, twists may be used for decoration (Fig. 22-1C). Ends have to go through punched square holes or be shouldered and rivetted in round holes. A fence consisting only of square bar uprights, with alternate ones twisted, could be sufficiently attractive. An alternative is to include scrolls (Fig. 22-1D) occasionally in the length of a fence. A scroll could fill the width of a space or be attached to only one upright.

The pattern of a fence can be broken by the inclusion of a badge, emblem, or initials at one or more points (Fig. 22-1E). Either forge what you want to insert or cut it from sheet steel. Use a fairly bold treatment and make it large enough to be seen from a distance. Weld all this between short rails, large enough to go over long uprights, and have short ones rivetted centrally.

Alternate the pattern with plain or twisted rods, which might stop at the top rail or be taken through and given decorative tops—either spear or leaf—or the split and spread pattern shown in Fig. 22-3K.

Decorative railings used to surmount a plain wood, brick, or masonry fence could be just a few inches high, or 15 inches or so, depending on how much you wish to increase the total height. The steelwork will obviously enhance the appearance of an otherwise characterless fence.

Unless the steelwork is exceptionally high, sections may be joined to each other and downwards into the main fence to support themselves, possibly with a gatepost at one or both ends.

Scrolls make good fillings for one of these fences. If all you need is a few inches of height, they can be horizontal (Fig. 22-2A). The frame is flat strip, with uprights of the same section between the scrolls. Allow for screws downwards through the bottom rail and through the ends into a post.

For a slightly deeper frame, the scrolls may be upright (Fig. 22-2B). As shown, the frame is made of flat strips and the uprights are square rods. The scrolls can be the same width as the uprights and not more than ³⁄₁₆ inch thick. Rivet or weld the scrolls in place.

A fencetop frame could have round and square uprights alternating. In this example (Fig. 22-2C), shoulder and rivet the uprights into the bottom rail. Take the round rods through the top rail and decorate the projecting ends. Simple points are shown. Twist each pair of square uprights in opposite directions.

As the problem of support is not so great, it would be possible to make these narrow

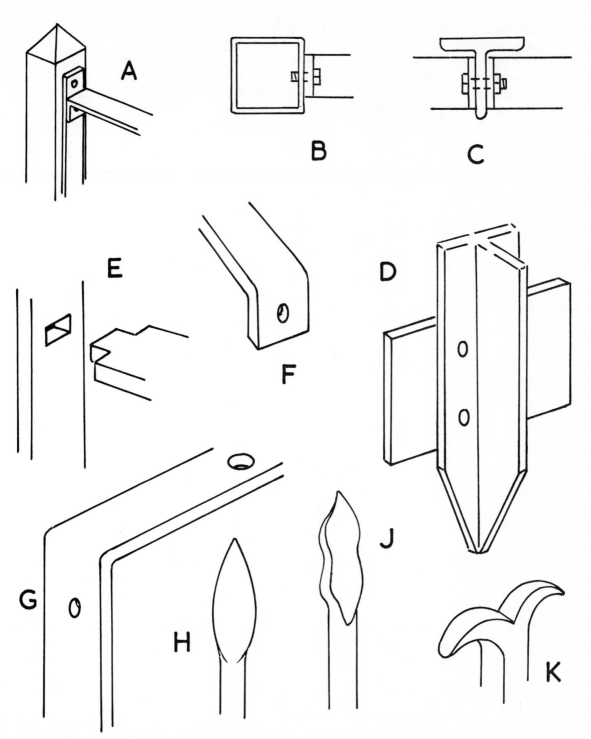

Fig. 22-3. Railing and fence parts can screw to posts. Joints can be tenoned. There are several ways of decorating the tops of rods.

115

railings fairly long. However, for convenience in handling 72 inches is about the maximum, and you will probably prefer 48 inches. Where an end comes against a post, it can be treated in the same way as the deeper fences. Where sections have to join, they can be brought together without posts for bolting through (Fig. 22-2D). If your design includes pieces projecting upwards, the meeting parts could also project for bolting (Fig. 22-2E). Include holes for screwing downwards at convenient positions.

23

Wheelbarrow

The common wheelbarrow with a single wheel is a versatile means of transporting a reasonable load, because it can travel along narrow paths or along planks, can be turned on the spot, and its load tipped where you want it. Making the framework is an interesting smithing project. Although it is possible to make a wheel, a purchased rubber-tired wheel is suggested because it is much easier to push. It might be possible to buy the container, although this can also be made from wood or sheet metal (preferably galvanized).

This wheelbarrow (Fig. 23-1) is a suitable size for most purposes. All the parts of the main frame can be made from strip 1¼ or 1½ inch wide. The thickness of strip will depend on how much hard use the barrow will get. For ordinary use around your yard, ¼ inch should be enough, but for very hard work you could use ⅜ or even ½ inch. Remember that these add to the basic weight you have to wheel. Parts may be joined with ⅜-inch bolts or screws, some with countersunk heads, although rivets could be used in some places.

Some frame sizes depend on the wheel, so get that first. A wheel about 14 inches over the tire is suitable. The part of the frame where it fits must have ample clearance. As drawn, with a 14-inch wheel, the barrow stands with the handles about 18 inches above the ground and 24 inches apart. If your wheel is very different or you prefer a different handle arrangement, modify the height of the legs.

The first step is the main frame (Figs. 23-2A and 23-3A). Start at the forward loop and work back symmetrically. If your strip is 1½ inches wide, reduce it to 1¼ inch for the handles, because this is the most that can be gripped comfortably by the average person. When you complete the barrow, rivet on wood cheeks to make round handles (Fig. 23-4A).

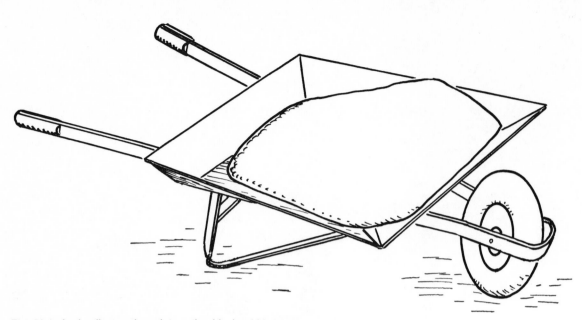

Fig. 23-1. A wheelbarrow is an interesting blacksmithing project.

Make a strip to fit across the forward part, with turned-down ends (Figs. 23-2B and 23-3B). Loosely bolt it in position.

The main supports and the legs are in one piece. Make it to fit across (Fig. 23-3C) and turn down squarely to the main frame (Fig. 23-2C). Twist each leg so you form a curved foot on it (Fig. 23-2D), then slope the flat strip up and over the piece loosely bolted in place. When you have checked that the shape is right and the opposite sides match, drill and bolt to the main frame and to the forward crosspiece. Cut off the ends high enough to provide support for the container.

While the parts are temporarily assembled, make and fit the bracket piece (Fig. 23-3D) between the leg. Take its ends as close to the twisted feet as possible. Its three connections can be rivetted. Drill for a bolt on which the wheel will pivot. Use washers or short tubes on each side to keep the wheel central. If the wheel needs a bolt axle thicker than 7/16 inch, thicken the sides with strips welded on to provide enough strength (Fig. 23-4B).

Whether the container is metal or wood, it can be held on with bolts or screws and washers through the extending front supports and the part of the leg assembly across the framework. Drill for three or four screws in each place. Take the assembly apart for painting, then bolt or rivet permanently in each position.

A suitable size for a container is shown in Fig. 23-5A. This is about the minimum size to suit the framework. You could increase it by a few inches each way, if you wish. The development shows how to cut sheet metal, with enough at the joints for rivetting (Fig. 23-5B). Use at least 14-gauge sheet metal and leave enough on the top edges to wrap over a piece of 1/4-inch round rod, taken all round to form a stiff rim. The sizes provide a guide to the shapes of wood panels, if that is the construction you prefer.

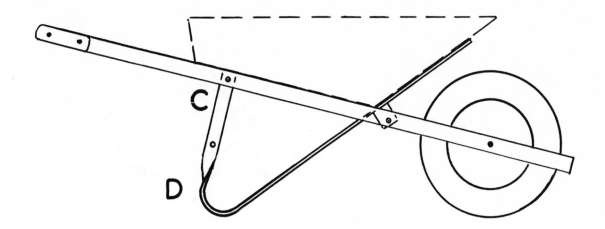

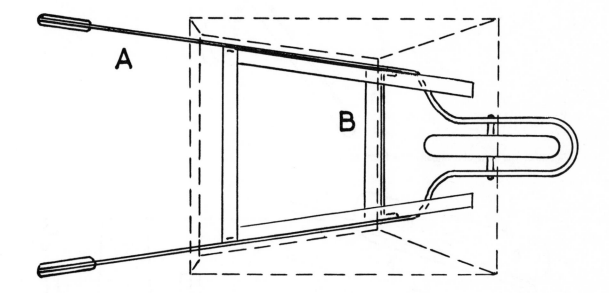

Fig. 23-2. Suitable sizes for a wheelbarrow.

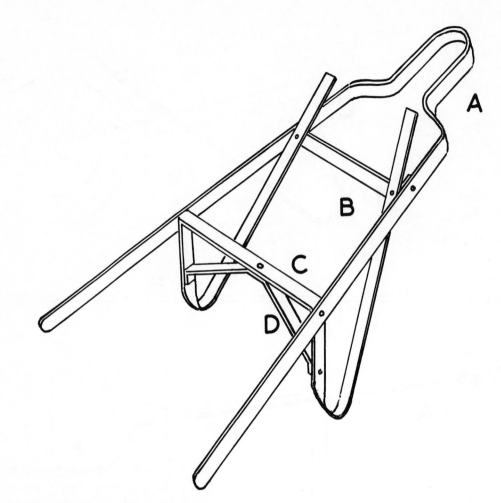

Fig. 23-3. The parts of a wheelbarrow framework.

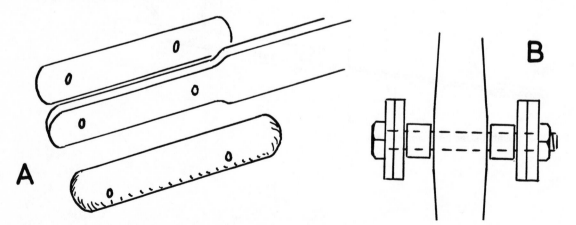

Fig. 23-4. Handle construction and the wheel pivot.

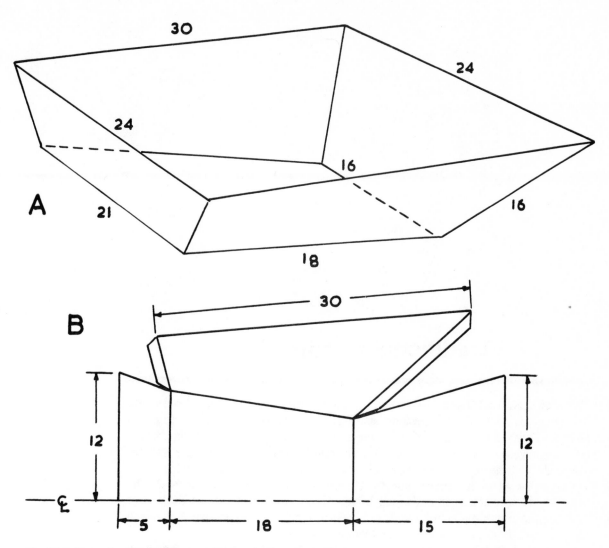

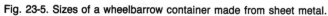

Fig. 23-5. Sizes of a wheelbarrow container made from sheet metal.

24

Traditional Candlestick

This project is included as a challenge to anyone who claims to be a skillful blacksmith. The project is based on a medieval design (Fig. 24-1), and is an opportunity to match your skill against that of a smith of many centuries ago. We have to use mild steel, where smiths of bygone days used iron, which has a marginally better capacity for fire welding. The making of the cage, in particular, tests your skill at your chosen craft.

Overall sizes are not critical, but suitable proportions are shown in Fig. 24-2. The main shaft is made of nine or ten ¼-inch diameter rods. The feet are ¼-inch thick sheet or strip. The drip ring is ⅛-inch sheet, and the candle holder is either a piece of ⅞-inch tube or made from ¹⁄₁₆-inch sheet rolled into a tube.

For the shaft, it helps to temporarily wire the rods tightly together, so they keep in a round bunch as you fire-weld one end. Remove the wire and fire-weld the opposite end. Have this part too long to start with. Heat the part that will form the cage, grip one end in a vise, and unwind by gripping the other end. There will have to be further heating while you manipulate the rods into an even shape with fine-jawed tongs or pliers. Be careful that the ends do not become reduced excessively and make sure they are kept parallel, at about ¾-inch diameter.

Cut the shaft to length and shoulder the ends to rivet through the base and drip ring (Fig. 24-3A). Check straightness and that the shoulders are square to the length.

Cut the base from ¼-inch sheet completely, or make two opposite feet and the center part as one, then weld the other two feet in place (Fig. 24-3B). Thin and roll back the tips of the feet (Fig. 24-3C), then curve the feet uniformly (Fig. 24-3D). Give the surface a grain marking by hammering with a chisel having a rounded, rather than sharp, end (Fig. 24-3E). Drill the center to take the shaft.

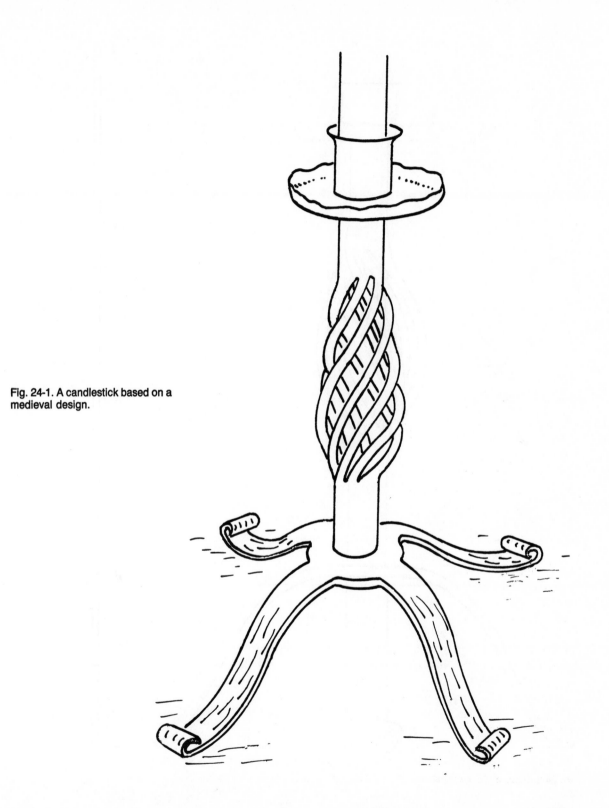

Fig. 24-1. A candlestick based on a medieval design.

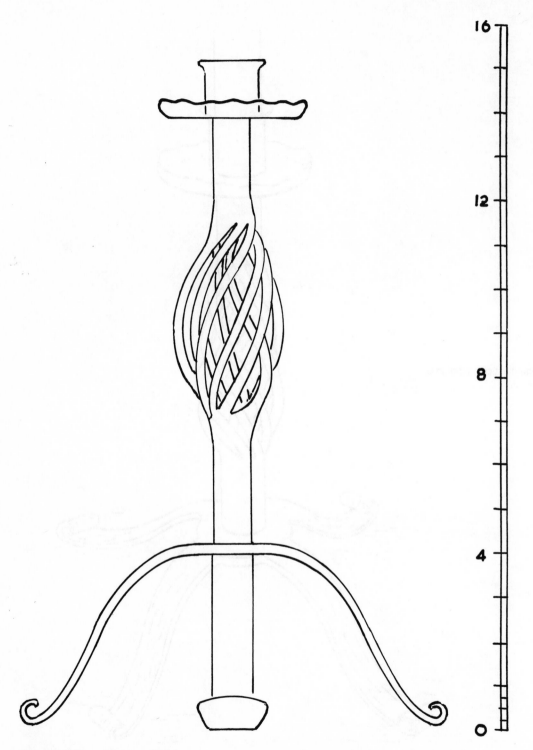

16

12

8

4

0

Fig. 24-2. Sizes of the candlestick.

124

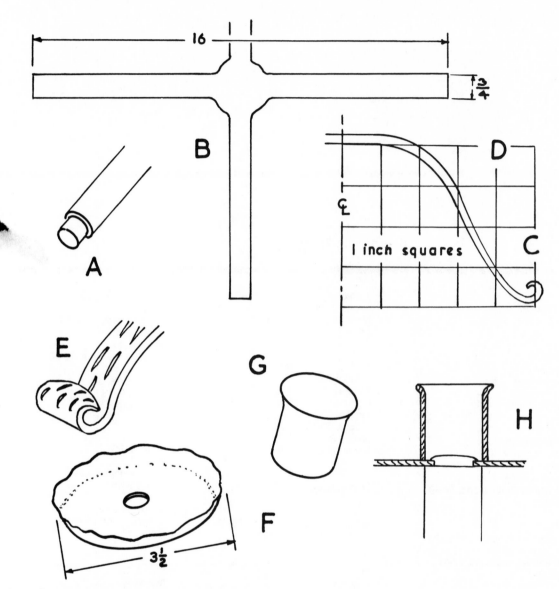

Fig. 24-3. Shapes and construction of candlestick parts.

Cut the disc for the drip ring (Fig. 24-3F). Dome it slightly. Final shaping of the deckle edge may be left until after doming, in case this process distorts the pattern slightly. Drill to take the shaft.

Check the size of the candle you intend to use. Most are about ⅞-inch diameter. Traditional candles were of uncertain diameter and a spike was sometimes used instead of a holder to cope with different diameters.

Make the tube and flare its top (Fig. 24-3G). Rivet the shaft to the base and the drip ring. Braze or solder the candle holder to the drip ring (Fig. 24-3H).

A black burnt-oil finish would be appropriate for this project.

Index